DATE DUE

Dec 16 70		
Jan 20 '71		
Oct 10 '73		
~~Nov 4 74~~		
Aug 3 '76		
Oct 6 '76		
May 22 78		
Nov 30 79		
Mar 22 '81		
Mar 2c '83		
GAYLORD		PRINTED IN U.S.A.

PUBLICATIONS OF
THE METROPOLITAN MUSEUM OF ART
EGYPTIAN EXPEDITION
VOLUME XVIII

The Sporting Boat

THE METROPOLITAN MUSEUM OF ART EGYPTIAN EXPEDITION

MODELS OF DAILY LIFE IN ANCIENT EGYPT

FROM THE TOMB OF MEKET-RĒ' AT THEBES

By H. E. WINLOCK

PUBLISHED FOR

THE METROPOLITAN MUSEUM OF ART

BY HARVARD UNIVERSITY PRESS

CAMBRIDGE · MASSACHUSETTS

MCMLV

© COPYRIGHT 1955
BY THE METROPOLITAN MUSEUM OF ART

DESIGNED BY BURTON J JONES JR.

LIBRARY OF CONGRESS CATALOG CARD NUMBER 55-5981
PRINTED IN THE UNITED STATES OF AMERICA

Foreword

Among the many discoveries made by Herbert Winlock during the years when he was conducting the excavations of the Metropolitan Museum of Art in the necropolis of ancient Thebes, perhaps the simplest and yet to him the most intriguing was the find which forms the subject of this volume. No difficulties of dating were involved, for to an Egyptologist so well acquainted with the necropolis its location alone would have been enough not only to indicate the dynasty during which the deposit was made, but even to identify the ruler whom its owner served. There were no problems of reconstruction such as confront the excavator who uncovers the scanty remains of a temple which for many generations has been used as a stone quarry. Here a few dabs of glue and bits of thread were all that was necessary to mend broken joints and torn rigging and to restore the models to their pristine state. The only inscriptions on any of the models were two examples of a text written in the clearest of hieroglyphs and repeating the commonest of offering formulas. Thus no questions could arise either in decipherment or in translation.

But in archaeology, generally, and not alone in epigraphy, there is a stage which follows decipherment and translation, and that is interpretation. The study of the models of Meket-Rē' involved neither of the first two stages, but the last Winlock attacked with all his vigor.

Our acquaintance with the daily lives of the ancient Egyptians is derived for the most part from their tombs. Their chief desire as they contemplated the life after death was to insure a repetition of life on earth, and they painted on the walls of their tombs pictures of their daily activities as well as of the provision and preparation of food, so that their souls in their visits to the offering chambers might enjoy and benefit from these representations. A device which supplemented such tomb pictures arose in the late Old Kingdom and became popular in the Eleventh Dynasty. This was the provision of miniature models depicting activities like those represented on the tomb walls. It is in this category that the models of Meket-Rē' belong.

In the literature of Egyptology there are two outstanding works dealing with ancient Egyptian life. One, Sir J. Gardner Wilkinson's *Manners and Customs of the Ancient Egyptians*, was published very nearly one hundred years ago. The much later work of Adolf Erman appeared in English translation as *Life in Ancient Egypt* in 1894. Both treatises are based for the most part on information derived from the tomb paintings.

The models of Meket-Rē' are a very considerable addition to the available evidence, for they are by far the most comprehensive group yet given up by the ancient tombs, and in them so many activities are represented in the greatest detail. Moreover, here there is no difficulty in interpreting either design or action as is so often the case in pictures because of the unaccustomed "perspective."

These factors were of course immediately apparent to Winlock, and the find was a sort of challenge to bring up to date the published information regarding Egyptian life. He accepted the task with enthusiasm, making a thorough study of each of the models and of the activities in which the men and women were engaged. There is no mention in his discussion of the sailing vessels of the fact that he rigged a round-bottomed boat with square sail and double rudder oars just to see how maneuverable the ancient ships were; nor has he included the fact that his inquiries into the ancient system of brewing beer led to his submitting the dry lees from beer jars to representatives of the brewing industry, one of the side results being the naming of an extinct yeast *Saccharomyces Winlocki* in his honor.

Circumstances, unfortunately, did not permit him to complete this painstaking research. Continuing excavation in the field, and then the call to the directorship of the Metropolitan Museum, left little time and energy for such activities. In the course of the years he did add many notes to his dossiers of various aspects of Egyptian life, but finally ill health forced him to give up the comprehensive treatment he had envisaged. Had it been otherwise the science of Egyptology would already have been much the richer. As it is, the full descriptions, the complete photographic record, and the careful drawings which form the bulk of

FOREWORD

this volume provide an accurate picture of many aspects of life as it was lived in Egypt in the Eleventh Dynasty. They will be of inestimable value to the future archaeologist who undertakes the task which Herbert Winlock was compelled to relinquish.

Had he been able to bring this volume to completion Winlock would have made acknowledgments to many persons with whom he discussed various problems arising from his consideration of the models. They must unfortunately remain nameless except for his immediate colleagues who assisted him, first in the field and later in the Museum.

The plans and drawings were made by Lindsley F. Hall and Walter Hauser except for Plate 55 which shows all the models in position in the *sirdāb*. This Winlock, himself, made as he removed them from the tiny room. The photography was the work of Harry Burton, who was also overseeing the excavations at the moment the models were found. The burden of putting the material into shape for publication was borne by Charlotte R. Clark who worked closely with Winlock during the entire composition of this book. In the latter task as well as in the removal of the objects from the tomb the undersigned was privileged to lend a hand.

AMBROSE LANSING
Curator Emeritus of the Department of Egyptian Art

CONTENTS

LIST OF PLATES

LIST OF PLATES

Introduction

Excavation is serious business for the professional archaeologist, and in consequence his official reports often seem, to the outsider at least, as dry as the dust he has to clear away in order to get down to what he's looking for. Winlock's Museum publications are more readable than some, but his attitude in them, as in his field work, was that of the scientist—to present the evidence and to draw such conclusions as seem appropriate.

For the general reader of his official reports it is perhaps unfortunate that he did not allow himself to stray from this prescribed course, for in conversation he could and did enliven the stories he had to tell with imagination and wit. As it happens, this story of the discovery of the funerary models so delighted some of his friends that he was persuaded by them to write it up for popular publication. It appeared in Scribner's Magazine for February 1921. So many years have passed since then that even the most interested of readers would have some trouble in looking it up. So it has seemed appropriate to reprint excerpts from that vivid account as an introduction to the somewhat more sober, even if extremely interesting chapters that follow.

Winlock called his story "Digger's Luck" and began it by speaking at some length of the very bad luck the Expedition had been having right through to the middle of February, that is to say, nearly the end of the normal digging season in Upper Egypt. But here is the story in his own words:

"I had gotten as far on my way home as the ruins of Medinet Habu. The walls of the old temple were turning pink in the sunset glow. The water-wheel that drones and quavers all day under the palms near by was silent for the night. Way up where the purple shadows were creeping out of the valleys in the tawny mountain I could see little specks of men and boys winding down the paths from the work at the tomb. The evening meal was being prepared and the bluish smoke of cook fires was beginning to float over Gurnet Murrai, where the tombs are seething tenements of Arabs and their flocks. At the house they would be getting tea ready and I was late.

"From the passers-by on the path there broke into my thoughts a cheerful voice saying: 'May thy night be happy.'

"I looked around and recognized one of our workmen, Abdullahi. 'And may thine be happy and blessed,' I replied, without checking my donkey, who was far more interested in getting home to his evening clover than in stopping for wayside greetings.

"But Abdullahi felt otherwise. He must shake hands—quite an uncalled-for politeness, I thought—and evidently wanted to stop and chat.

" 'I am going home,' he informed me, and I said that that seemed evident. 'And when I get my blankets I am going back to spend the night at the tomb.' For the life of me I couldn't remember whether we kept guards up there at night to look after the equipment, but I supposed we must, and as I started on again I laughingly hoped he had something to watch. 'The Headman Hamid says I must tell no one, but your Honor will see something up there,' Abdullahi called after me.

"He had charged his voice with all the mysteriousness he could put into it and his whole manner would have been strange enough to impress me at any other time, but I was convinced of failure, and when I remembered that Abdullahi belonged to one of the gangs which were clearing those corridors, I knew perfectly well there could be nothing to it all. Daressy had surely dug those corridors out, and our reclearing to draw a plan could not possibly show up anything new.

"At the house I met Lansing and Hauser coming out. They said they were going up to the work, and showed me a scrap of paper with a hastily scribbled note from Burton: 'Come *at once* and bring your electric torch. Good luck *at last*.' This seemed preposterous. Surely it was another false alarm, and we had had so many of them. However there

2

was Abdullahi and his mysteriousness, and I decided to let my tea wait a while and go with them, but I refused to have any hopes, and the three of us got ready all sorts of sarcasms for Burton's benefit as we trudged along.

"A little knot of Arabs was standing around the mouth of the tomb in the twilight. Inside in the gloom we could just make out Burton and the head men. There was something in the air that made our sarcastic remarks sound flat. Burton pointed to a yawning black crack between the wall of the corridor and the rock floor. He said that he had tried to look in with matches but they didn't give light enough and told us to try the torches.

"At least a hole here was unexpected, but we had looked into so many empty holes. Anyway, I got down flat on my stomach, pushed the torch into the hole, pressed the button, and looked in.

"The beam of light shot into a little world of four thousand years ago, and I was gazing down into the midst of a myriad of brightly painted little men going this way and that. A tall slender girl gazed across at me perfectly composed; a gang of little men with sticks in their upraised hands drove spotted oxen; rowers tugged at their oars on a fleet of boats, while one ship seemed foundering right in front of me with its bow balanced precariously in the air. And all of this busy going and coming was in uncanny silence, as though the distance back over the forty centuries I looked across was too great for even an echo to reach my ears.

"I was completely stupefied when I gave my torch to the others and one by one they looked in through the crack. It was almost night now and we saw that we could do nothing until the morning. While the other two went back to the house to get sealing-wax and cord, Burton and I sat down dazedly to talk it over. He told me how he had been coming down from the mountain-top, where he had been taking photographs and had stopped at the work to dismiss the men as usual. As he expected, they had cleared most of the fallen stone from the corridors, but just before he had come along one of the men in this one had noticed that the chips had an unaccountable way of trickling into a crack as fast as he dug. At first the man hadn't paid much attention. It was just one of those crazy whims of the Americans that had made them want to dig out such a place anyway. Still he had called the head man of his gang and together they were scraping away the stones from the crack when Burton had arrived.

"When we left the tomb for the night the crack was stopped up with stones and stretched across with strings securely sealed with sealing-wax—quite a little of which was on my fingers. The gang which was working in the corridor had received all sorts of needless instructions about keeping some one on watch all night. None of them slept a wink for the next three nights, I am sure, sitting in the starlight in front of the tomb discussing the baksheesh they hoped to get. We were no less excited. That night we sat up late discussing what the place could be and each one of us dwelling at length on some marvel he alone had seen. I believe some one claimed to have seen Santa Claus and his eight tiny reindeer—or possibly I dreamed I had seen him. Anyway, I for one woke up in the morning with a raging headache that was made no better by trying to seem masterfully calm.

"In the morning our work began, and three terrific days followed. Burton rigged up mirrors to throw sunlight down the corridor and took a photograph of the crack in the rocks. Then we dug in front of it and found in the floor of the corridor a little pit, about a yard square and waist-deep. It had been carefully filled with chips of the very rock it was cut in, and both ancient thieves and modern archaeologists had taken this filling for the living rock of the mountain and passed over it. The side of the pit under the wall of the corridor was built up of mud bricks, and when we had photographed them and taken them away we were looking down into a little low chamber about three yards square and scarcely four feet high into which no man had entered for four thousand years. Rock had fallen from the roof—in doing so it had opened up the crack we had looked into the night before—and had upended one of the boats and broken others, but except for this nothing had been disturbed. Our only fear was that as fresh air got into the chamber more would come tumbling down, and we were torn between a desire to get everything out safely before we had a catastrophe and to get a complete set of photographs and plans of everything just as we had found it. It was just luck

4

that made both possible, for after we were finished tons of rock began to fall in the tomb. Still we escaped the misfortunes of our French colleagues digging half a mile away. They had a man killed by rock falling in a tomb chamber while we were working in this one.

"We photographed, we planned, we carefully cleared away chips of fallen stone, and then we lifted out one or two of the boats or a group of little men and began all over again. One night will always remain a weird picture in my mind. Lansing and I had gone up to clear away more of the fallen shale to get ready for Burton's photographs in the morning. From afar off we began to halloo to the guards, for we had lent them a couple of revolvers and we were afraid of the zeal they might show in their use in the dark. Duly challenged, we made our way up the slope and inside the tomb, and lit candles to work by. For hours we worked away, the shadowy Arabs pattering barefooted back and forth from the flickering candle-light out to the open, where the brilliant desert stars seemed to hang right down to the mouth of the gloomy tunnel.

"As we worked along through those three days and nights we began to realize what it was that we had so unexpectedly discovered. The tomb was that of a great noble of four thousand years ago. He himself had been buried in a gilded coffin and a sarcophagus of stone in a mortuary chamber deep down under the back of the corridor, where the thieves had destroyed everything ages before our day. Only this little chamber had escaped and it was turning out to be a sort of secret closet where the provision was stored for the future life of the great man.

"He could not conceive of an existence in which he would not require food and drink, clothing and housing, such as he was used to in this life, and being a rich man, naturally he wanted an estate in eternity like that which he had owned on earth. His philosophy carried him beyond that of the savage chieftain who expects a horde of servants to be slaughtered at his grave. He attained the same end by putting in his tomb a host of little wooden servants, carved and painted, at their daily tasks, working before little portraits of himself. The spirits of these little servants worked eternally, turning out spirit food or sailing ships upon a spirit Nile, and his soul could enter any one of the little portraits of himself at

5

will to reap the harvest of their labors. In short we had found a picture of the life the great noble hoped to live in eternity, which was nothing more or less than the one he had led on earth forty centuries ago.

"The first thing we had seen when we had peeped through the crack had been a big model nearly six feet long, showing a noble seated on a porch among his scribes, taking the count of his cattle as they were driven past. In the back of the room we found, under a lot of other models, neatly stacked, the stable where these same cattle were being fattened, and finally when we came to move one big boxlike affair in the far corner—a model I had tried my best to get a peep into and almost fallen headlong in the process—we found it was the butcher shop where the cattle's life history ended. The night we worked in the tomb by lamplight we got a peep into a granary where diminutive scribes sat writing down the quantity of grain being measured and carried to the bins by hardworking laborers. And later we ran across the bakery where the grain was ground and made into loaves and the brewery where the home beverage was being fermented in tall crocks and then decanted into round-bellied jugs. Lansing extricated two canoes manned by fishermen who hauled a miraculous draft of painted wooden catfish and perch in a seine, and I picked the fallen stones out of two gardens in which copper ponds—that would hold real water—were surrounded by little wooden fig-trees and cool, shady porches. Then there was a carpenter shop and another shop where women spun thread and wove cloth. The very threads on their distaffs and spindles—frail as cobwebs though they were with age—had remained unbroken in that eternal stillness.

"The business of the great man entailed a lot of traveling, and his idle hours were passed in pleasure sails or fishing trips on the Nile or on the still backwaters of the marshes. On the celestial Nile he would want to go voyaging or yachting, too, and therefore a dozen model boats were put in the chamber. We found them setting sail, the captain bossing the sailors who sway on the halyards and set the backstays. A man throws his whole weight against the pole as they put off from the bank and another stands by in the bow with a fender in case they bump against another vessel. When they travel down-stream against the north wind the

6

mast and sail are lowered and the crew man the sweeps. The noble himself sits under the awning in front of the cabin smelling a lotus flower
while his son sits on deck beside him and they both listen to a singer and
an old blind harper. Inside the cabin squats a steward beside the bunk, under which are shoved two little round-topped leather trunks. A kitchen-
boat follows, and the cooks get ready a meal to be served when evening
comes and they are moored to the bank. There were yachts, to be sailed
with the wind or paddled against it, and a low raking skiff, from the bow
of which two men are casting harpoons while others land an enormous
fish over the side.

"Thus had the great man lived and so did he expect to live after he
had gone to his 'eternal abode,' as he called it. Finally, the funeral day
had come. His body was brought across the river from his mortal home
in Thebes, through the green fields where the wondering peasants
leaned on their hoes to watch it pass, and then up through the rocky
gorges to his tomb. A long procession followed him, each model borne
on the head of one of his serfs, and a crowd of peasant girls and women
from his estates brought baskets of wine and beer and baked meats for
the funeral banquet. Even their contributions were expected to go on for-
ever, and statues of two of them, half life-sized, had been made to go with
the models in the chamber. There we found them, towering above the
hord of miniature men and beasts, looking over at us with grave, wide-
open eyes. Four thousand years they had stood thus silent—if only we
could have broken that silence and got from them the secret of the pattern their tightly clinging dresses were made on, we were sure we could
have made a killing in the suit and clothing trade in the New York of
today.

"Four thousand years is an eternity. Just saying it over and over
again gives no conception of the ages that have gone by since that funeral.
Stop and think of how far off William the Conqueror seems. That takes
you only a quarter of the way back. Julius Caesar takes you half-way
back. With Saul and David you are three-fourths of the way, but there
remains another thousand years to bridge with your imagination. Yet in
that dry, still, dark little chamber those boats and statues had stood in-

7

different to all that went on in the outer world, as ancient in the days of Caesar as Caesar is to us, but so little changed that even the finger-prints of the men who put them there were still fresh upon them. Not only finger-prints but even fly-specks, cobwebs, and dead spiders remained from the time when these models were stored in some empty room waiting for the day of death and burial. I even suspect that some of his grandchildren had sneaked in and played with them while they were at that house in ancient Thebes, for some of them were broken in a way that is hard to explain otherwise. Possibly that is a wild guess, but at any rate there is no doubt of what had happened to them in the little chamber in the tomb on the day of the funeral. After all of the models had been stowed away and the masons had come to brick up the doorway, they had found one of the boats in their way. So one of them picked it up and laid it to one side on top of the granary, and under bow and stern he left a great smear of the mud he had just been mixing for mortar. There those smears still remain.

·   ·   ·   ·   ·   ·   ·

"The little models had to be parted after all these ages together. Half of them went to the Egyptian Government, under the terms of our concession, and are now on view in the museum in Cairo. The others can be seen in the Metropolitan Museum in New York. If any reader should see them there in their glass cases he will get a far better first view of them than we did with our electric torches flashing through that crack in the rock—but none of us would swap places with him. They meant too much to us that evening when we were wondering where we would dig next."

A. L.

I

THE TOMB
OF MEKET-RĒʿ

ABOUT 2000 B.C.[1] there died in Thebes a great noble named
Meket-Rēʿ. He first appears on the monuments about 2022 B.C. as one of
the party who accompanied King Neb-ḥepet-Rēʿ Montu-ḥotpe on a voyage up the Nile to the Shaṭṭ er Rigāl when the king went there to meet
In-yotef, the heir to the throne, and the Chancellor Akhtoy on their re-
turn from a journey into Nubia. On the rocky wall of the little valley at
the Shaṭṭ, Meket-Rēʿ had his name cut as the "Truly Beloved of his Lord
and Governor of the Six Great Tribunals." [2] It was probably a few years
later that his name was written among those of the courtiers in the king's
mortuary temple at Deir el Baḥri as an "Overseer of the Chancellery," [3]
and then followed several years during which he acquired many other
honors. As we learn from a comparatively small number of fragments of
relief from the walls of his tomb, he was "the Hereditary Prince, the
Count, the Treasurer of the King of Lower Egypt, the Hereditary Prince
at the Gateway of Gēb, the Great Steward, the Sole Companion and the
Chancellor." [4]

9

When first we meet Meket-Rē' during the reign of King Neb-ḥepet-Rē' he bears titles which suggest that he was already a man forty or fifty years of age, and a score of years later he must have attained his allotted three score years and ten, or thereabouts. By that time the Chancellor's son, also called In-yotef, had already been made a "Treasurer of the King of Lower Egypt," and Meket-Rē' himself had long been anticipating the grave. Ever since the succession of King Se'ankh-ka-Rē' Montu-ḥotpe in 2010 B.C. he had obviously been spending great wealth, and probably much of his own time, on the preparation of a tomb near that of his new master. The spot which he chose for it was under the Theban mountain, overlooking the place set aside for the king's own tomb. Stonecutters, sculptors, and painters must have labored there in numbers, and even the models which are the subject of this book obviously came from several different workshops. Probably Meket-Rē' had had objects for his future life made throughout the years of his prosperity.

Originally the tomb of Meket-Rē' was the most imposing one in the Eleventh Dynasty cemetery at Thebes,[5] but located as it was behind Sheikh 'Abd el Ḳurneh hill and thus hidden from the cemetery watchmen, it was eventually plundered by robbers and quarrymen of the late Middle Kingdom or of the early years of the New Kingdom. Today there is nothing for the visitor to see there, but when the tomb was first completed it must have been one of the great sights of the necropolis (Plate 54). It was situated on the south side of a mountain spur which overlooked the valley bottom, and the hillside was graded for a length of over 75 meters and a width of nearly 30 meters. A mud-brick wall 160 centimeters, or 3 cubits, thick fenced in this sloping causeway, which ascended from a gateway at the bottom of the hill. The orders of Meket-Rē' seem to have been to make the causeway some 50 cubits wide and about 140 cubits long. The lower left-hand (southwest) corner of this approach had to be quarried out of a little rocky knoll, and in the boundary wall at this corner three gaps were left to serve as entrances to little tombs, of which, however, only one had been completed. At the top of the causeway another small tomb was cut into the rock on the left, and on the right was the tomb of the Steward Waḥ,[6] with a small brick offering chamber built above it. A second small crypt beside that of Waḥ had been made to contain embalming materials.

At the top of the causeway a flat space about 7 meters wide was cut at the foot of the cliff, and since the native limestone rock was far too fissured to give sculptors any chance to display their abilities in such material, there was built across the tomb façade a portico of "proto-Doric" columns painted to imitate granite. The walls of the tomb were faced with fine white limestone and must have been exquisitely carved, to judge from the fragments we found. In the center of the façade was the doorway to a corridor which went straight back into the mountain nearly 20 meters. At the end of the corridor was a square chapel, with a niche at the back to house a statue of the deceased, and beneath the chapel floor, a hidden pit leading to the burial chamber. A curious feature of this tomb is a second corridor, chapel, pit, and burial chamber of the same proportions as those of Meket-Rē‘, cut out just to the west in the same portico and so arranged that the pit leading to the burial chamber would be respectfully a little to the rear of Meket-Rē‘'s. Without much question it was started later than the burial place of Meket-Rē‘ himself but certainly before the latter was completed. A cross passage connected the two chapels, presumably as a convenience to the mortuary priests who were to perform the services in them, and also, probably, to assure an entrance to the tomb of Meket-Rē‘ for the soul of his son In-yotef, who was undoubtedly the owner of the second tomb. Whether In-yotef was actually buried in this tomb is, however, open to question. Within little more than ten years after the funeral of Meket-Rē‘ [7] Thebes was abandoned as the capital of Egypt in favor of It-towe, just south of the head of the Delta. Since the actual burial chamber provided for In-yotef yielded us nothing whatever in the way of antiquities, it may be argued that he followed the court and that his tomb in Thebes was never occupied. However, a few fragments of models, one bearing his name, were found in the rubbish in the tomb, and it is possible that he was actually buried there and that plunderers thoroughly ransacked his burial place.

The tomb causeway and the portico were open to all, and even the sculptured corridor and the statue chamber were probably entered by ancient visitors, on feast days at least. Naturally, no one could get to the sealed burial chamber, which was, as custom dictated, behind and below the stela, in front of which the services for the dead were performed. In the burial chamber with the coffin of the deceased was placed the requisite funerary equipment. But in the Middle Kingdom it was customary also for the wealthy person who could afford it to include in his tomb little models of his house, his workshops, and his boats, with his servants performing their tasks, in order to assure the continued satisfaction of material wants and the repetition of pleasures enjoyed on earth. To accommodate these models, an additional small chamber was often provided, not too far from the burial chamber and, like it, sealed and hidden from anyone who was bent on thievery or wanton mischief. This was an outgrowth of the very early idea of putting a statue of the owner in a special secret chamber—a *sirdāb*, as the modern Arabs call these little rooms—and of the addition later of a few figures of servants preparing food and drink for him eternally. In Meket-Rē''s tomb there were two such *sirdābs*, one belonging with his own crypt, for in it were models with inscriptions containing his name, and the other doubtless for his son's benefit.

The *sirdāb* which probably belonged to In-yotef was entered from a little pit dug midway between the entrances to the two tombs in the floor of the portico and against its rear wall. The pit was a very rough little hole, about 120 centimeters square at the top and no more than 120 centimeters deep. It had been so placed beside the foundations of the rear wall of the portico that the bricks blocking the doorway came just under the sandstone footing of the wall. Inside this doorway there was a little passage which led to the *sirdāb*, a room about 250 centimeters long and slightly narrower, in which one could not stand upright. Ancient thieves had plundered it, and in 1895 Daressy found it, as we also did in 1920, absolutely empty.[8]

Fortunately for us, the *sirdāb* of Meket-Rē' remained untouched (Plates 2, 3, 54, 55), and his name was inscribed on two of the objects in it. We were the first who had had any inkling of its existence for almost forty centuries, thanks to the fact that the chips filling its entrance pit came from the very rock in which the pit itself had been cut. This pit was an extremely rough hole, about half way along the left-hand side of the corridor of the tomb. It measured only about 125 centimeters square and the same in depth. The rock in the neighborhood of the tomb is half way between a limestone and a shale and is so friable that a good job of cutting it is impossible. However, being fissured and shattered, there is no difficulty in quarrying it, if one is content to follow its bedding, and so the pit was not at right angles with the corridor, the little chamber going off at an angle. The room itself was about 3 meters square but so roughly quarried out that no dimensions can be more than approximate. In height it was from 125 to 150 centimeters before some of the ceiling just inside the entrance collapsed.

Into this small chamber had been crowded no less than eight house models, twelve models of boats, two large figures of offering bearers and a group of four small ones, and an enormous scene of Meket-Rē' inspecting a parade of his cattle (Plates 4–7, 55). Whether these models were brought to the tomb and deposited in their *sirdāb* at some time before Meket-Rē''s death and burial, or whether they formed part of the funeral cortege is uncertain, but I am inclined to favor the latter view. The condition in which we found them and the way they were stored in the *sirdāb* will be discussed later; at the moment reference to the plates will be sufficient.

When all the models had been put into the chamber the mason started building a wall across its entrance to seal it up (Plates 2, 3). Workmen had already brought unbaked mud bricks, 34 x 17 x 8 centimeters in size, to be laid in mud mortar which was prepared and waiting. As the mason laid each brick he spread a handful of mud on top at each end and laid the next course in these pats of mud. After five courses had been laid in an orthodox way, with alternating headers and stretchers, the next five courses of stretchers were run up leaving a wide empty space in the center of the wall. Into this, broken bricks were dumped in any fashion. By now the mason was within three courses of the top of the doorway, and he eked out his bricks with bits of stone and narrowed the course from inside. It was a good, strong wall, easily able to withstand the pressure when the pit itself was filled. The corridor floor was paved with sandstone slabs which completely hid the *sirdāb* pit from prying eyes, while the filling of the pit prevented any hollow sound from giving away its presence. The filling drifted into the chamber only as the bedrock which formed the lintel of the doorway began to collapse. This happened when quarrymen removed stones from the corridor during later dynasties, knocking off the top of the brickwork sealing up the entrance to the chamber below.

For almost four thousand years the models stood in this dark little chamber in which not a breath of air moved except when an occasional piece of stone fell from the ceiling. Then, on the 17th of March, 1920, our workmen unexpectedly disclosed the existence of this miniature world which had remained a secret for so long.[9] In the years that have passed since then, many references have been made to these models of Meket-Rē', for they are without question the most perfect set ever unearthed in Egypt.[10]

The twenty-four models fall naturally into three groups. One of these relates to the estate of Meket-Rē': his residence and the various buildings used to provide him with the necessities of life. A second group consists of bearers of offerings. The third is a remarkable set of river craft which emphasize the importance of the Nile both as a highway and as a source of food.

The individual models are described in this order in three separate chapters, which are followed by a discussion of the group as a whole. In the Appendix appears the catalogue of the models and here are listed the technical details such as dimensions, construction, condition when found, and the repairs which had to be made in the case of those which were damaged.

1. In this book it is assumed that the XII Dynasty began in 1991 B.C. (Winlock, *The Rise and Fall of the Middle Kingdom in Thebes*, p. 91.)
2. Winlock, *Excavations at Deir el Baḥri, 1911–1931*, p. 118.
3. Winlock, *ibid.*, p. 19; Edouard Naville, *The XI Dynasty Temple at Deir el-Bahari*, Pt. II, pl. IX, D.
4. Winlock, *Rise and Fall*, p. 67. Some of the fragments are in the Metropolitan Museum, Acc. nos. 20.3.162, 163; 31.3.2, 3, and others unaccessioned.
5. Winlock, *Deir el Baḥri*, p. 17, fig. 2, pls. 24–30.

6. Winlock, *Deir el Baḥri*, pp. 29, 222, pl. 30.

7. Winlock, *Rise and Fall*, p. 67.

8. G. Daressy, *Annales du Service des Antiquités de l'Égypte*, II (1901), p. 135. He was obviously in error when he wrote that this chamber contained the embalming materials. In 1920 we discovered the latter in the little crypt just outside and below the east end of the portico, where they had always been.

9. Winlock, *Bulletin of the Metropolitan Museum of Art*, December, 1920, Pt. II, pp. 12–32; *Deir el Baḥri*, pp. 17–30, pls. 24–30.

10. See for example, in addition to those already referred to, *Ancient Egypt*, 1921, Pt. II, p. 64; Winlock, *ibid.*, 1922, Pt. III, pp. 71–74, Fig. 2; *Journal of Near Eastern Studies*, Vol. II, No. 4, Oct., 1943, p. 281, Fig. 1, Pl. XXXIX; H. Ling Roth and G. M. Crowfoot, *Ancient Egypt*, 1921, Pt. IV, pp. 97–101, frontispiece, and Fig. 2; C. H. Johl, *Altägyptische Webestühle und Brettchenweberei in Altägypten* (Untersuchungen zur Geschichte und Altertumskunde Aegyptens, Bd. VIII), 1924, pp. 10 ff., Taf. II, Abb. 45; James Henry Breasted Jr., *Egyptian Servant Statues*, 1948, passim.

I I

THE MODELS

OF MEKET-RĒꞌꞌS ESTATE

1. THE RESIDENCE. MODELS A AND B.

THE RESIDENCE of Meket-Rēꞌ is represented by two models, one of which fell to the lot of the Cairo Museum in the division of antiquities at the close of the excavations, while the other is now in the Metropolitan Museum in New York (Plates 9–12, 56, 57). They are to all intents and purposes identical, except that in the Cairo model a few details have been carried a little nearer to completion. The New York model had been placed where large sections of the roof of the *sirdāb* fell into it, damaging the trees to such an extent that they had to be removed in order to repair them. The interior of the model was thus completely exposed to view, and we were able to photograph not only the entire façade of the porch but even its ceiling.

The model is in no sense a complete representation of Meket-Rēꞌꞌs residence, for only the wall separating the interior from the garden is in-

cluded. The interior details are indicated by the surfaces of two doors
and a latticed window, carved on the exterior back wall of the model.
Each is painted red to show that it was made of wood. The central door,
the great front door of the house, is double valved and has an elaborate
fanlight above it, designed, after the fashion of modern Arab mushrebiyeh,
to let cool air into the house through its innumerable little openings while
at the same time keeping out the blazing Egyptian sunlight. The fanlight
is made for the most part of *djed* signs, with two bunches of lotus flowers
above, the whole arranged in a style which goes back to the beginning of
the Old Kingdom and was particularly popular at this period—the early
Middle Kingdom. Below the fanlight are the two valves of the door, each
elaborately cleated on the inside, with hinge pivots at the top and bottom
of the upper and lower cleats. There is no groove marking the place
where the two leaves of the closed door meet, but at a convenient height
an elaborate lock with a single bolt is carved in high relief. On the outside—the porch side—the doors are left plain except for horizontal in-
cised lines extending across the bottom. The smaller, single valve door
at the right of the main door may be a less important entrance to the
house, or it may equally well represent a door between two rooms in the
interior. The very tall, latticed window with narrow openings on the left
of the main door would not let more than a dim light into the house but
it would admit cool breezes. These three openings are all that there is to
suggest the interior of the residence: shaded windows and high fanlight
to let air into the dwelling, but a front door tightly bolted against
intruders.

The house is represented as made of unbaked mud bricks plastered
over with yellow desert clay, the typical construction of all such buildings in Thebes. The walls of the porch are decorated with a broad black
dado, above which is a frieze of blue, yellow, and white bands, topped by
a wider white band; the low wall across the front is painted white to show
that it was made of limestone. The porch has a flat roof whose low front
parapet is pierced by three rainspouts, painted white to imitate limestone.
These are long enough for the streams of rain water which might issue
from them to fall into the pool in the garden below and not drip into

THE MODELS OF MEKET-RĒ''s ESTATE

the porch. The spouts in the Cairo model are actually pierced so that water could run through them, but those in the other lack this touch of realism. In the porch there are two rows of four slender wooden columns, carved and brightly painted, which rest on white bases. The rear row simulates clusters of papyrus stalks and the front row, lotus buds bound together with gaily colored bands of red and blue. The wooden architraves which they support are bespangled with stars, and the wooden ceiling between them is carved to represent palm trunks split in two, brightly painted with stripes of green and red. This was the typical ceiling construction in houses of the period.

Beyond the porch the garden wall is painted with stripes like those on the porch, but is dropped lower than the walls of the house itself. This was doubtless to show that the level of the garden was a little below that of the porch, but in both models the garden and the porch floor are actually on the same level. The master of the house, seated in the shade of the porch looking out over the garden, would be cooled by the breeze coming across the pool—clearly the reason for this design of the ancient landscape architect. In each model the pool takes up the entire center of the garden, but in real life we have every reason to suppose that the garden itself was much larger. The sloping sides and the bottom of the pool are lined with copper, obviously so that it might be filled with water. Around the pool welcome shade is given by trees, and there can be no doubt as to what kind of trees they are meant to be. On no Egyptian tree except the sycamore fig does the fruit grow directly from the trunk and the main branches, and that is the tree which is represented here. Trunks and branches are painted green, the leaves a lighter, bluer green, and the figs reddish brown.

2. CATTLE BREEDING ON THE ESTATE.
MODELS C, D, AND E.

The most outstanding model, both for size and for originality of subject, is the one which shows the inspection of cattle on the day when they were counted, and doubtless registered for tax purposes (Plates

13–16, 58). For a great landowner this was obviously one of the important events of the year. The scene is laid in a place on Meket-Rē"'s estate where he, with his retainers gathered about him, could overlook the proceedings from a pavilion. In front of it is a part of the wide cattle yard, which was surrounded by a wall too high for any beast to escape or for anyone to look over it. Only the portion of this wall at the back of the pavilion is shown in the model. The floor of the pavilion was probably about a meter above the level of the yard and was reached from the left by a flight of steps. Thus Meket-Rē' and those with him were assured of a safe vantage point from which to watch the cattle passing in front of them. The roof of the pavilion rests on four columns which have papyrus capitals and stand on bases, painted white to imitate limestone, set in gaps in the low parapet at the front. On the edge of the roof there are two long white rainspouts to carry the rare rain water far out into the courtyard. Obviously this is not the garden porch beside the pool, although built in much the same style as the residence. This pavilion is somewhere else on Meket-Rē"'s estate.

Meket-Rē' himself is seated on a formal, old-fashioned throne in the middle of the pavilion, and his son, In-yotef, sits on the floor at his left, resting his elbow on his knee. To their right there is a row of four scribes, seated as In-yotef is, each with a roll of papyrus on his lap and a pen in his right hand, busily writing down the number of cattle as they are counted (Plates 15, 16). In front of the scribes, lying on large chests in which the documents will eventually be filed, are their writing palettes, the ink cakes within easy reach. To the right and left of this central group are some of Meket-Rē"'s retainers; one stands beside In-yotef, another is at the opposite end of the platform next to the scribes, and at each end of the pavilion, down in the yard itself, two other men stand ready with their long staves either to beat off obstreperous bulls or to chastise any hapless cowhand who may arouse the master's ire. These retainers wear kilts painted white to represent linen, those on the men with the staves being long enough to reach down to their calves. On top of the painted kilts in many cases is a bit of real linen, draped in the same fashion. All these men have smooth-shaven heads and light yellow complexions, showing that they belong to the leisured, educated class. Clothing, complexion, and shaven heads differentiate them from everyone else in the scene with one exception. In the yard below is another man of their class, standing between two sunburned cattlemen, the three of them keeping count of the animals driven past, on the fingers of their two hands. Whether this man is Meket-Rē''s own scribe or whether he comes from the government to take account of the cattle for the tax collectors, it would be hard to say, but having two cattlemen checking on the scribes' count lends a touch of realism to the scene.

The model represents the exact moment when one of the cattlemen, doubtless the leader, has stopped below the pavilion to bend his knee respectfully and to bow his back in homage, while he touches his left shoulder with his right hand by way of salute to Meket-Rē'.[1] The very humble crossed their two arms over their breasts, touching both shoulders at once.[2] In the model, in addition to the leader, there are ten more cattlemen, who lend a boisterous and realistic animation to the scene by officiously beating the animals to make them move faster past Meket-Rē'. All of them are clearly men used to an outdoor life; they have great mops of hair covering their heads like turbans, to ward off the sun's rays which otherwise might strike them down,[3] and each is burned a deep rich brown where their skins are exposed. Presumably they are yelling at the beasts as they drive them past Meket-Rē', who calmly watches from his seat on the pavilion. Two sturdy fellows armed with heavy clubs belabor the animals to make them form a single file as they hustle by the three men who are counting them.

With a little imagination we can hear the resounding whacks of the clubs wielded by the cowherds as they fall on the backs of the beasts. One hopes that they are well padded with fat. Some animals are not only beaten; they are also led with ropes tied around their horns or, in the case of one big black animal, by a rope tied around its lower jaw where the man leading it can give a most painful tug, if it ever shows signs of getting fractious. These animals are either bulls or cows, for there is no evidence of there having been any oxen in ancient Egypt. In spite of the long horns they were probably not very dangerous animals, for if we are to trust the scale as the model shows it, few of them could have stood more than a meter high at the shoulder. Food cattle were far smaller than the great, massive bulls which hauled stone on sledges.[4] In color they go all the way from jet black or solid red to piebald beasts with spots of both colors, and even to a pepper-and-salt breed with little black spots all over them.

In the next chapter of their story, the cattle of Meket-Rēʿ are in a stable being fattened for slaughter (Model D; Plates 17, 59). The model of the stable, like all the estate models, is represented as being plastered with yellow clay and with doors and door frames painted red to show that they are made of wood. The doors turn on wooden pins which fit in holes in long cleats fastened to the wall above and in sockets cut in the sills below. This is the only instance where the doorsills are painted red; in all the other models they are painted white to represent limestone. The back half of the stable is a big stall, doubtless thought of as being roofed, with one long wall entirely taken up by a manger, its white color indicating the material of which it is made. In this stall four already plump animals are eating until there is danger that they will never be able to get through the rather small door which connects the stall with the rest of the stable. In all probability the front half of the stable is a yard and was left entirely unroofed. At least that seems to be the arrangement in later stables. Here the animals are given their final hand stuffing before being led to the butcher shop. One of the two animals can still stand, but the other has had to lie down. The cattlemen seated in front of them tug at cords tied around their lower jaws to make them open their mouths while little balls of food are tossed in for them to chew. They eat through force of habit only, but they still have a long way to go, for beside the men is a model of an enormous basket of grain and a pile of straw, represented by a rough block of wood painted gray, which still have to be consumed. By the entrance door of the shop sits a doorkeeper, with his scepter of authority, ready to stop intruders or to prevent the escape of animals from the stable. The beasts themselves look too fat and lazy to harbor any such thought, and it is far more likely, therefore, that the doorkeeper is there to guard against any unauthorized person entering

the stable. The three larger animals in the stall and the one that is standing in the yard are black or black with white spots, while the small calf
and the animal lying down are plain red.

The butchering of the cattle took place in a shop which was one of
the largest and most interesting buildings on the estate of Meket-Rē'
(Model E; Plates 18, 19, 21, 24, 60, 61). The model shows that it had a
large front room with a ceiling even higher than the two stories which
formed the back of the premises. The whole shop was completely roofed,
the roof sloping down from front to back. Apparently this roof was made
separately so that it could be removed, and it is so shown on Plate 18. To
let in air, the main room is open across the upper part of its front wall
and two wooden columns, set on bases let into the top of this wall, support the front architrave on which the roof rests. Two thicker, full
length columns on wider bases, painted white to represent limestone,
support the architrave in the middle of the room, and two smaller columns, like those in front, set into the parapet along the balcony at the
rear of the shop, support the third architrave. All these plain cylindrical
columns are painted red to represent wood. The entrance to the shop is
through a door in a side wall near the front of the building. A stairway
diagonally across from the door goes up to the balcony where joints of
meat hang from two lines strung from one side to the other in the coolest
and airiest part of the shop. Under the balcony there are three doors
opening into a long undivided space which was empty when we found
the model. It is to be assumed that these doorways led into three separate
storerooms, but no partitions had been put into the model, and when
it was placed in the *sirdāb* all the doors were shut. Apparently Meket-Rē'
knew what was supposed to be behind the doors.

In the shop everyone is busy under the watchful eyes of two men
who hold wooden scepters in their right hands. One stands near the entrance door with the end of his scepter resting on the shoulder of a man
who holds a bowl to catch blood gushing from the slit throat of a bull.
Perhaps he is chastising him for some carelessness, but more probably it is
mere chance that the scepter is in that position. The other overseer stands
at the bottom of the balcony stairway. He has a writing palette under his

left arm and holds a roll of papyrus, painted white, which probably contains a list of the animals to be slaughtered.

At the moment there are only two animals in the butcher shop, both trussed up and lying on the floor being slaughtered. One has a plain red hide and the other is piebald black and white, and both have all four feet tied together.[5] So tied, the animals have been easily thrown on their sides, and the butchers, wearing short kilts spattered with blood, grab the beasts' muzzles with their left hands and haul their heads around, stretching their throats before cutting them with the knives held in their right hands. Meanwhile, men sitting opposite the butchers hold bowls to catch the blood which comes spouting out of the animals' throats.

Bigger bowls of blood are cooking over two circular braziers tended by men who sit beside them with fans in their hands, blowing up the fires. In the model these braziers are of two different designs. One has an upper rim which rises into four points on which the bowl rests, leaving openings through which the fire can be fanned. The design of the other brazier is somewhat different, for there are no crenelations around its top, but a little door at the bottom of one side makes it possible to tend the fire. One brazier is painted red and the other black, doubtless to show that real braziers were made of clay hardened by the heat inside, one even to the point of turning it red. Fans were probably made of the leaves of *dōm* palms. Finally, there is a man sitting near the door plucking the feathers from a pintail duck which he holds by its wings. The striking thing about this man is that his skin is sunburned a dark red and his hair is long and bushy, in contrast to the rest of the men in the shop, who have shaven heads and the lighter complexion of the more sheltered classes. Perhaps this duck plucker is a more menial servant than the butchers, while everyone else in the shop is of the scribe, or effendi, stratum of society.

The cuts of beef hanging on the lines on the balcony show how very different were the practises of the ancient Egyptian butcher from those of modern times, in Chicago, for example. The biggest cut is a rib roast, so severed from the rest of the carcass as to extend far forward into what today is called the chuck, and probably back into the loin and rump. In other words, practically the whole side of the animal was cut off in one piece. Another cut was the round, with the two ends of the hip bone pro-jecting. The most numerous of all the cuts, however, are long strips of boneless tenderloin, or other parts of the animal sliced into triangular bits to look like tenderloins. These last slices make up three-fourths of the joints on the lines, but all the meat hanging there accounts for just about half the cuts. We know that at funeral banquets a foreleg—usually the right one—was cut off in one piece to be offered to the dead or to the god.[6] Furthermore, the tenderloins are shown as being far too large and too numerous to have come from the same animals that provided the ribs and joints from the shoulders. However, the chances are that the model makers felt that the cuts shown would be easily recognized by the soul of Meket-Rē', for it is very unlikely that any ancient Egyptian could be ig-norant of so common a scene as the cutting up of a beef.

3. BREAD AND BEER MAKING ON THE ESTATE. MODELS F AND G.

Every ancient Egyptian estate of any size had its own granary, from which grain was drawn as it was needed.[7] Grain was the common medium of exchange, and when necessary everything could be reduced to terms of so many bushels of barley or spelt, even though such reckoning often meant elaborate and tiresome calculations. Good harvests were the very essence of Egyptian economy: plentiful crops spelled ease, short crops meant famine. Safe storage bins were necessary to protect these crops, and the granary was the treasury for the greater part of the riches of the Nile valley. In practically rainless Egypt there was no need for roofing the granaries, and even today the *shūneh* of the modern Egyptian is open to the sky.[8]

One of the characteristics of the present-day Egyptian granary is that it usually has the outer walls peaked up with slightly rounded crene-lations at the four corners. It is just such peaks that we see on the four corners of Meket-Rē''s granary (Model F; Plates 20, 21, 24, 62, 63). The entrance has a cleated door, its upper hinge support tied in place with cord. Just inside is a long vestibule running the whole width of the build-

25

ing, and at the far end of it a second door, its hinge support pegged to the wall, opens into a stairwell with steps leading up to a broad walk atop a partition wall between three storage bins. These bins each have a round-topped doorway below for the removal of the grain, and we must presume that each opening could be closed with removable planks, omitted in the model. When deposited in the *sirdāb* all three bins were probably filled with actual grain, and in two of them there were also put rough blocks of unpainted wood representing piles of grain, just like the similar block in the cattle stable. However, when we found the granary there was very little in the bins except these blocks and a few husks remaining after mice had finished eating the real grain.

The personnel needed to run this granary numbered at least the sixteen men whom we see at work, and who are obviously the minimum in an establishment of this size. In the first place, there is the doorkeeper, squatting at his post with his scepter in hand. He wears his hair long and is sunburned too dark a brown to be taken for one of the class of scribes. Near him sit four scribes, each with smooth-shaven head and light complexion, who are keeping count of the baskets of grain as they are carried up to the bins. Two of them are writing on large wooden tablets, painted white to imitate the plaster with which such boards were often covered. These lie across their knees with their pen cases on them. The right hands of the scribes are carved as though they held brush pens, although these are not provided in the model and the tablets are perfectly clean. Between these men is a large white jar for water to moisten the ink, smudges of which are represented on the outside. Two other scribes sit opposite the first pair, each with his left knee raised and with a scroll of papyrus across his lap, partly unrolled, referring to the records written on them. In front of each of these men is a square document box with a cleat across its lid to serve as a handle, and on them are laid the writing palettes which are liberally bespattered with ink where the pens have been tried out. Under the outstretched finger and unquestionably under the watchful eye of an overseer who stands near the door leading to the bins, two laborers measure the grain. This overseer and another man seated cross-legged on the floor opposite him are both of the scribal class, as their light, unsunburned complexions and their shaven heads indicate. On the other hand, each has thrown one corner of his kilt over his shoulder like the porters, as if they too might take a hand with the grain sacks at any moment. Of the peasants with bushy heads of hair, one squats near the group of men at the back of the vestibule, and we may take him for a farmer who has just delivered grain, or more likely as a peasant keeping count of it on behalf of his fellows. Beside him two thick-haired men fill a bushel measure and pour its contents into sacks which are then carried off by half a dozen sturdy fellows, each of whom wears a corner of his kilt thrown up over his shoulder as a protection from the rough sacks. Through the door and up the stairs they toil, and when they have reached the broad walk above the bins they dump the grain to them.

The wheat, barley, and other grain must each have had its own household bin in the kitchens of the residence of Meket-Rē', whence small quantities could be drawn as needed. Many kinds of grain could probably be used both for making bread and for what the Eleventh Dynasty Egyptian obviously looked on as a related household task, the brewing of beer. In 2000 B.C. baking and brewing started out in the same way, the risen dough in one case being cooked and in the other, soaked in water and fermented to make beer. Thus bakers and brewers share one building in Meket-Rē''s models (Model G; Plates 22–24, 64, 65). It is a somewhat elongated structure, divided down its length by a fairly high partition wall, making two rooms in which the servants are engaged in the two occupations. A door through the partition wall near one end connects the rooms. Each room has a roof partly covering it lengthwise. Such a roof does not appear to be unreasonable, but it is always possible that the rooms are shown only partly roofed so as to permit observation of the activities going on in the model. The entrance to the shop is through a door at the left of the brewery half of the model, and this opens into a little vestibule where the doorkeeper sits at his post with scepter in hand. He is shaven headed and light complexioned, as are all the other men at work in this building. Straight ahead of him is the brewery, and to his left through a doorway he can also keep an eye on the bakery.

Since both baking and brewing started with the making of dough

2 7

containing yeast to make it rise, the first thing needed was flour, and the first step in grinding flour was to crack or crush the grain with pestles on flat limestone mortars laid on the floor. In the brewery half of the model a man labors at this task with a large wooden pestle which tapers to a slender handle at the top and swells to a broad bottom, probably as much as fifteen centimeters in width on an actual pestle (1, on Plates 64, 65). In the bakery three men wield similar pestles. Each blow of these flat-bottomed implements would crush or split any grain in the mortar and make it ready for the women who grind it into flour. Two of these women are so occupied in each half of the shop. They wear white, knee-length shifts which leave their arms free, and their long hair is gathered back behind their shoulders so that it will not fall into the mills as free-hanging tresses would. Their hand mills are practical even if very primitive affairs (2). The bases are painted black, probably to represent Nile mud, and they are high at the back where the women stand, the top sloping forward so that the ground flour will run into a catch basin in front. The model millstones are of unpainted wood, which is about the color of the real gritstone ones, and they are being rubbed back and forth by the millers. It is somewhat curious to find that the most tiring work in the shop is being done by the only women in it. However, the mixing of the dough was a pretty strenuous job, too. This is carried out by two men standing at their vats in the bakery, but in the brewery one man stands waist deep in a vat, holding on to its rim, as he mixes the dough by treading it with his feet.[9] The vats are represented as being tall red pottery vessels liberally smeared around their upper edges with the overflow of white dough (3).

In the brewery half of the shop the next task is to shape the dough into rough little cakes which are then allowed to rise. There is enough yeast in a little old dough mixed in with the new to leaven an entire batch in the course of a day or so, and probably old dough was kept over in a flat, black tray which is on the floor near the dough mixer (4). Perhaps a splash or two of light color in the tray represents some of this crude yeast. A man stands beside a tall, round, white mixing-table shaping dough into cakes, which he sets aside to rise (5). The cakes of risen dough were then mixed with water to make a fermenting mash in barrels (6).[10] Each barrel is identical in size and shape with the vat in which the dough was mixed and is painted to imitate pottery, though of a somewhat lighter color than the vat. Filled with crumbled up bits of risen dough and with water, they would stand open to the air for a short time, and then their contents would be dipped out with a jar and poured into four larger pots which stand in a row along the opposite wall. Three of these pots have already been filled and stoppered, the sealings being large lumps painted black to show that they were made of mud (7), and the jar being filled will soon be sealed in the same way (8).

In the bakery things are even busier than in the brewery. This half of the model is divided into two small rooms by a low partition wall, and in each room cooks are at work. After the flour is ground the dough is mixed in vats by two men whose hands are covered with dough (3). The dough is put into two lighter colored vessels, like the fermentation tubs in the brewery, which are placed beside the two cake makers in the inner room of the bakery (6). One of these men is working up a long, slender loaf from a lump of dough (9), and his mate, using a slightly larger board, has made five little round buns and two larger four-cornered loaves (9).[11] The baking is done in four ovens, painted black to represent clay, each of which has an attendant who pokes the fire through a little square door below and probably throws handfuls of fuel on it to keep up the blaze. The two circular stoves in the back room are low braziers (10), much like the one with the flat top in the butcher shop; the ovens in the outer room are tall and square with sloping tops, and above the fire door there is a semicircular door into the oven where the bread goes (11). A basket filled with conical loaves, the long thin tips of which have been baked a rich brown, stands on the floor of the outer room (12).

4. THE SPINNING AND WEAVING SHOP. MODEL H.

Whoever made the spinning and weaving model was hardly a skillful sculptor, but he seems to have known every step in these crafts from start to finish so fully that he was able to give an excellent representation

29

of them (Plates 24–27, 66, 67). The model shows that this shop on Meket-Rē''s estate was one large room, at both ends of which there was a roof just wide enough to cast a shadow over the working ends of the two looms. Between these roofs the shop is open, but it is hard to say whether this was the common design of weavers' shops, or whether it was merely done here to let us look into and admire the model. There is not a single man in the whole establishment, and it is fair to assume that in Thebes, at the outset of the Middle Kingdom at least, spinning and weaving were looked on as women's crafts. In the New Kingdom both men and women are shown in the weaving shops.

The first thing the women have to do is to prepare slivers, or roves, as spinners call the lengths of loosely twisted flax fibers, which are obtained when the stalks are soaked and retted. Three women, clad in simple white shifts, sit in a row along the wall near the door of the shop, getting these roves ready for the spinners (Plates 26, 27, 67). Each woman has her right knee tucked under her and her bared left knee raised so that she can roll the fibers together on it. In front of each woman is a heap of flax fibers, represented by a block of wood irregularly speckled over with paint. At first the women let the single-ply rove accumulate in a pile in front of them, and there it lies, represented by real linen thread, but every once in a while these long roves are wound up into balls which lie on the ground in front of the women. In the model these balls are of wood, but there can be no question that each is supposed to represent loosely rolled yarn.

The next step is to twist three roves into a single thread, and for this purpose three balls of yarn are placed in each of the pots which stand on the floor behind the three spinners. In the model these pots are solid bits of wood, painted red outside and white on top, and from a hole in the top come three roves, here of real linen thread, which are not yet spun together. Actual pots were made of pottery or limestone and had rings inside through which the roves were run to keep the balls from jumping out of the pots. The spinners have wrapped the roves around wooden spindles, just under the whorls, which are held at arm's length in their left hands. Between these spindles and others held in their right hands there is a single thread which has been spun by the second spindle. On this second spindle, thread previously spun has been wound just under the whorl. The spinner on the right in Plate 26 (bottom) stands with both feet on the ground, winding the finished thread onto the spindle in her right hand and getting ready to spin some more. The two spinners on the left have finished winding and have raised their right knees to roll the spindles rapidly along their bared thighs, in order to make them rotate when they are dropped and hang at the end of the spinning thread. This twists the three roves into one thread, and the women, with their two feet on the floor again, will wind it on the spindle and be ready to repeat the whole operation.

When the spinners in Meket-Rē"'s shop had wound as much thread as possible on their spindles they gave them to two women for making the warps on pegs driven into the wall. Some of the real threads on the pegs when we first found the model had already been broken, but photographs taken before it was moved show them as depicted in Plates 26 and 27. The two women are winding the warp threads on groups of three pegs in such a way that when they are transferred to the beams of the loom the alternate threads will cross each other, thus making the necessary two sheds. Thus, in the weaving each shot of the shuttle will lay a weft thread above one half and under the other half of the warp threads. Little or no thread remained on one set of warping pegs. On the other set, however, enough was left to show that the model maker did not take the trouble to wind the warp so that when it was transferred to the loom the alternate threads would cross to make the sheds; [12] it is merely wound round and round the pegs, and if taken off, would have no crossing in it at all.

The thread having been spun and the warp set up, everything is ready for the women who work the two looms. Each of these women wears a simple white shift with only one shoulder strap, a dress not tight enough to prevent their sitting on the floor with both knees raised and their skirts hanging down between their legs. The third woman at the loom nearest the door sits on the floor by the warp beam, probably to loosen it and unroll the warp as the other two weavers roll the finished cloth up on the breast beam. She can easily turn around when she has finished at one loom and be ready at the other; thus no more than five women were needed to work a pair of looms quickly and easily.

Both looms in this model are solid wooden affairs, shown flat on the floor of the shop (Plates 27, 66, 67). On each loom a length of cloth already woven, painted plain white to represent linen except for a fringe drawn along one side, is shown rolled up on the breast beam. This beam is a little way from two loom pegs driven into the floor, to which pegs it is clearly supposed to be lashed by ropes which can be tightened or loosened whenever the warp needs drawing up or letting out. At the opposite end of the loom the pegs are driven into the floor inside the warp beam, which must have been lashed to them, because if it had been left loose, it would have revolved and the warp threads, which are here shown going around it, would all have fallen slack on the floor. Beyond the finished cloth the loom is filled by what in reality must have been almost two meters of yet unwoven warp threads, represented by parallel black lines drawn close together, one after another, on the white board which represents the loom. On the far side of the heddle rod the lines are slightly staggered and are crossed by a yellow line which indicates where the one set of warp threads rises from below the other set. On every half dozen or so of the black lines, where they cross the warp beam, there is a horizontal black line which might be taken as a thread laced in and out of the warp threads to keep them evenly spaced. However, since there is a similar dotted line across the already solidly woven part of the cloth which is wound around the breast beam, we should probably take both these black lines as merely representing the outlines of the two beams of the loom, seen vaguely through the cloth and the as yet unwoven warp.

The chief weaver sits at the end of the loom behind the breast beam. Her assistant sits at the side, facing her, with one hand on the heddle rod and in the other hand a bit of wood, painted to look like limestone. With this stone she has just knocked the jack out from under her end of the heddle rod, causing the other jack to topple over. The jacks which belong to both looms lie on the floor beside the ends of the heddle rods, and the slings which hold up each alternate warp thread to those rods have presumably fallen through the warp. Now a slight raising of the second, slender rod—the shed stick—whose ends project on either side of the loom, will permit the shuttle to be thrown through the counter shed so created, and another weft thread will be in place. Raising the heddle rod on the jacks again will produce the shed necessary for the next shot. Whether two shuttles are being used by the weavers at the same time it is hard to say. Two shuttles exist, one in the chief weaver's hand and the other lying on the warp threads, both a little longer than half the width of the loom. However, it is possible to think of one of them as the shuttle used to weave the fringe on the edge of the cloth, while the other was used for the cloth itself. Finally, the gigantic beater-in—or sword—lies between the two layers of warp threads for the weavers to pull firmly toward the breast beam and thus drive the weft thread down after every shot of the shuttle. One end is pulled by the chief weaver, who sits facing the loom, and the other end is pushed by the woman who has just knocked out the jacks.

5. THE CARPENTER SHOP. MODEL J.

In the last of the models of Meket-Rē''s shops one can almost hear the rasping of the ripsaw as its teeth cut through a timber, the chopping of the adzes, the tapping of mallet on chisel handle, and the grinding of sandstone planing blocks. Altogether there are a dozen carpenters busily laboring at their tasks in his carpenter shop for the soul of Meket-Rē' (Plates 24, 28, 29, 68, 69). The greater part of the shop is an open court without any fixed feature except a rough wooden post set solidly upright in the middle for the use of the sawyer. The back of the court is sheltered under a narrow roof, which slopes a little toward the rear to protect the men who are at work there.

The sawyer's post is a tall piece of hard wood, chopped out roughly, to which has been lashed a squared piece of pine wood which the sawyer is ripping into planks. The rope with which the wood is tied in place is fastened with a simple knot, which can be readily loosened when the saw reaches it, and the lashing then raised or lowered as needed. The

33

sawyer has thick hair and his skin is burned a dark red. He is using an exceptionally large saw, which is like shorter ones stored in the tool chest.

Sitting on the floor around three sides of the shop are eight men dressing timbers with adzes and smoothing the roughly chopped-out planks. Some of these men wear their hair long and others have shaven pates, but there is no distinction between the tasks they perform. One piece of rough pine timber lies on the floor beside the shop door, where two men are at work on it, apparently dressing it square with their adzes. Along the wall opposite the door three men labor at the same task, dressing a heavier beam in the same way, while across from them sit three other carpenters, polishing down a timber with blocks of wood representing sandstone, which served the same purpose as planes and sandpaper in present day carpentry. On the floor in the middle of the shop lie two heavy planks pegged together with two hard wood dowels, the ends of which have not yet been cut off. We can only suppose that the planks lie there waiting for this to be done, after which they will be dressed with an adze to an even thickness.

Since Egyptian joinery depended on dowel pegs or on mortises and tenons to fasten planks together, it is perfectly natural to find one of the carpenters cutting a tenon slot in the edge of a plank which he is going to join to a second board. He has set the timber up on edge and sits on top of it, straddling it and holding a mortising chisel in his left hand while he pounds it with the wooden mallet held in his right hand. He has already finished one slot and has moved along the edge of the plank to cut a second in the middle. When that is done he will turn around to cut the third slot in the end of the timber where he is now sitting.

Finally, under the little roof in the far corner of the shop, three men sit around a small forge. The man in the middle keeps the fire up with a blowpipe, the original probably made of pottery because the smaller end, which he holds in his mouth, is painted a light buff color, while the somewhat larger, bulbous end which goes into the fire is blackened as if with soot. The forge consists of a firepot for charcoal, which sits inside a little black furnace partly covered over by a slab of lighter color. In the front of the pot is a small round hole into which the man tending the fire puts his blowpipe. The reason for roofing this end of the shop may have been to help control the draft and keep the fire at the right heat. The men on either side of the fireman are doubtless re-tempering tools which have been heated in the forge. In front of one man there are a light colored bowl, a square dark object something like the yeast tray in the brewery, and two roughly egg-shaped articles, the purpose of which is difficult to explain.

These artisans had a supply of spare tools which they kept in a big chest at the back of the shop. The lid of the chest was securely tied on, and over the knotted cord was a lump of soft clay, in which had been pressed a typical Middle Kingdom seal bearing a central device of two entwined scrolls. We were able to withdraw the knob on the front of the box and thus remove the lid without breaking the seal. Inside we found extra carpenters' tools, which we took out, and we then replaced the lid. These tools included axes, adzes and extra adze blades, saws, mortising chisels or reamers, ordinary chisels, and bow drills. The axes have large copper blades lashed into wooden handles with linen cords.[13] The extra copper adze blades exactly duplicate those lashed in place on the adzes with their wooden handles, and they were obviously provided as spares, to be used when the mounted blades became dull.[14] These adzes are just like the ones the carpenters are using. The saws are only about two-thirds as long as the ripsaw being used by the sawyer; they have wooden handles, and their copper blades have teeth more or less irregularly indicated along the cutting edge.[15] The ordinary chisels have blades which are square in cross section, the cutting edge flattened and presumably sharpened,[16] but the mortising chisels or reamers have a narrow cutting edge and an extra thick blade, which will not bend when chips of wood are pried out of deep and narrow holes.[17] The bow drills have long wooden shafts, rounded on top where they enter the drill sockets; they vary a good deal in length and have bits of copper, square in section and with a flat, sharp edge.[18]

1. The chief herdsman well illustrates the words of Ptaḥ-ḥotpe, who advises that whenever one meets someone "better than thou, bend thine arm and bow thy back," and in the tale of the Shipwrecked Sailor there is a passage

about how "I made answer to him, my arms being bent in his presence." (See A. Erman and A. M. Blackman, *The Literature of the Ancient Egyptians*, pp. 56, 32.)

2. A Middle Kingdom statuette formerly in the Carnarvon Collection and now in the Metropolitan Museum (M.M.A. 26.7.1393) has the arms in this position. See also Percy E. Newberry, *Beni Hasan*, I, pls. XIII, XXX.

3. Winlock, *The Slain Soldiers of Neb-ḥepet-Rḕ Mentu-ḥotpe*, p. 9.

4. Joints of beef from the tomb of ʿAshayet showed the animals to be 120 cm. high at the shoulder, while the work bulls bred to haul stone to the temple of Ḥat-shepsūt were much taller and more massive. (Winlock, *Deir el Baḥri*, pp. 45, 73.)

5. This was not the invariable practise, for there are many pictures of animals with only three legs hobbled together and with one foreleg left loose to be cut off at the shoulder, but at Thebes also we later found a painted wooden model of a young slaughtered animal, trussed up like Meket-Rḕ's, dating from just about the same time. The model animal was found in the forecourt of the tomb of Khety (Service No. 311) and is now in the Metropolitan Museum (26.3.103). Ancient pictures are innumerable.

6. A right foreleg of beef was found with other food offerings beside the coffin in the tomb of Waḥ (M.M.A. 20.3.258). See p. 10 above and Winlock, *Deir el Baḥri*, p. 29.

7. Winlock, *Deir el Baḥri*, pp. 58 ff.

8. According to Reginald Adams, Esq., former manager of the National Bank of Egypt, even the granaries of that bank are not usually roofed over, except perhaps in the far north near the sea. In fact, wheat, maize, lentils, and beans have been found by the bank to do best in the open air, unless the storage space can actually be hermetically sealed, when cereals may be kept in sacks for as long as a year. It is only in private storehouses, which will hold less than 500 *ardebs*, that age-long experience has proved that a closed granary is practical.

9. This thorough mixing seems to be confined to the brewing art, for the action is depicted in the wordsign for brewer (see Alan H. Gardiner, *Egyptian Grammar*, A 37 in Sign List). A.L.

10. One of the steps in brewing *bouza* in modern Egypt is to bake loaves lightly before crumbling them up and mixing with water into mash, but in this model the cakes of risen dough were obviously not cooked at all, for if that had been the practise in Thebes during the Eleventh Dynasty, there would be an oven in the brewery, even if it duplicated those in the bakery. It is improbable that anything as important as an oven was left out of the model by accident.

11. These are just like the actual loaves of bread found in contemporary foundation deposits (see Winlock, *M.M.A. Bulletin*, 1924, Dec., II, p. 10, fig. 6).

12. As in the reconstruction of another weaving model of the same period,

THE MODELS OF MEKET-RĒ''s ESTATE

M.M.A. 30.7.3 (see Charlotte Clark, *M.M.A. Bulletin*, Summer, 1944, pp. 26, 27 and illustrations).

13. Lengths 12 cm. One (a selection of these tools went to the Metropolitan Museum, the remainder went with the chest to the Cairo Museum, *Livre d'entrée* 46722)—M.M.A. 20.3.91.
14. Lengths of blades, 6 cm.; of handles, 9 cm. Two—M.M.A. 20.3.95, 98.
15. Lengths 13 cm. One—M.M.A. 20.3.92
16. Lengths 8.5–9 cm. One—M.M.A. 20.3.94
17. Lengths 8 cm. One M.M.A. 20.3.93
18. Lengths 15.5–18.5 cm. Two—M.M.A. 20.3.96, 97

III

THE FIGURES
OF OFFERING BEARERS

WHEN the ancient Egyptian set forth on his journey to the next world he had to be provided with food, drink, and other household equipment which had been necessary in mortal life. Therefore, Meket-Rē''s models included figures of men and women carrying in his funeral procession baskets of food and drink, a libation vase and a censer with which to perform the daily ceremonies at his table, and a pile of linen sheets with which to cover him in his unending sleep. Two half-life-size statues of girls bearing offerings are among the chief models which Meket-Rē' had in his tomb and were one of the first things to catch the eye when we looked into the *sirdāb* (Plates 4, 5, 30). They stood there, facing each other, in the midst of the crowds of diminutive figures filling the little chamber. A small procession of men and women carrying offerings belongs among the less painstakingly carved figures, although they too, like their big sisters, are still almost as fresh as the day they were made.

Far larger in scale than the figures in any of the other models were the two girls carrying baskets of offerings on their heads and holding

39

ducks in their right hands (Models K, L; Plates 30, 31). The figure on the left in Plate 30 is now in the Cairo Museum, the one on the right in New York. The girls are walking along sedately, each with her left foot forward, upon paths obviously representing black Nile mud, since the tops of the pedestals are painted black. However, the sides of the blocks are painted red, like the doors in the shops and all other parts of the models representing wood, probably because it was realized that these pedestals were merely reproductions. The skin of the girls is painted light yellow; their eyes and eyebrows are black, with just a touch of red in the corners of the whites of the eyes; and their finger and toe nails are white, outlined in red. Their hair is fancifully painted blue to show that it was not quite black, but this blue has changed to a dark green with time. We are to understand that both girls had dark brown locks, but brown is a color rarely used by the Egyptian artist, who often depended on blue to take its place.

Each girl wears a tightly fitting dress, supported by straps over both shoulders. Around her neck, wrists, and ankles she has a collar, bracelets, and anklets of brightly colored beadwork. All these ornaments are supposed to be made of rows of red, green, yellow, and blue cylindrical beads, with stripes formed of little ring beads between them. The dress of the girl now in Cairo is made of white linen, over which there hangs a red and green net of cylindrical and ball beads, making a series of zigzag chevrons. The girl in New York wears what may have been a dress of blue linen with narrow white stripes running up and down the lower part of the skirt, but its color has changed with time to a dark green. The upper part of the dress is covered by an elaborate beadwork garment in which the scalelike elements are colored blue, red, green, and yellow, outlined in white.[1]

On her head each girl holds a square basket, whose sides flare out slightly at the top, keeping it in place with her upraised left hand. These panniers are painted yellow to represent the reeds of which they were made, the individual reeds outlined with red lines, and the framework on which they are woven indicated by black bands around the edges and crossing in the middle of each side of the basket. The Cairo girl has four

40

tall red jars in her basket, each 25 centimeters high and stoppered with a conical lump of clay decorated with white spirals. The girl in the Metropolitan Museum carries an identical basket filled with meat and bread. At least it seems to be so filled. Actually, a false bottom supports samples of the offerings which are supposed to fill the entire basket from bottom to top. Across the basket lies the foreleg of a beef, skinned down to the shin joint, the gristle at the shoulder painted pink, the meat below red, and the hide on the unskinned part spotted black and white. In one corner of the basket lie four ribs of beef, not yet cut apart, colored red with white lines between them. A red beef heart stands upright in the opposite corner. A joint of beef for roasting is also painted red with the white ends of the bone showing at either side. There are two flat white loaves of bread—one round and the other triangular—in the middle of the basket, and at one side lie four slender conical loaves. Each loaf is slightly flecked with black near its pointed end to show that it has been well baked. Four flat, elongated objects with pointed ends lie in pairs, three of them painted blue and the fourth purple. They might be cuts of meat but are more likely some kind of vegetable, perhaps squashes or melons—it is difficult to say which.

Each girl has caught a live duck by its wings and carries it in her right hand. The duck held by the girl in Cairo has brown feathers on its back and on its breast white ones with pale blue shadings. Its wings are brown with black and white markings; its pointed tail is yellow with black details; and its bill and legs are black. The duck being carried by the girl in New York has a light brown back; its breast, wings, and square tail are white with brown stripes; and its bill and legs are red.

Few, if any, ancient Egyptian offering bearer figures are better than these two, but every collection contains some examples, for throughout the Middle Kingdom the fellow townsmen of Meket-Rē' would have a wooden statuette of a girl bringing offerings to the tomb, if they could afford one.

The third offering bearer model from the tomb of Meket-Rē' is a group showing a procession of two men and two women, walking along in step with left foot forward and with left hand raised to support whatever load they are carrying on their shoulders and on their heads (Model M; Plate 32). The pedestal on which the four figures stand was painted with yellow ochre, which must have been varnished on top, for now it is a bit darker than the sides. The two men have shaven heads, and they wear short white skirts. The first man has thrown a corner of his kilt up over his shoulder to protect his skin from the heavy vase he is carrying, just as the men filling the bins in the granary did to protect their shoulders from the sacks.[2] Both men are painted a reddish brown which was covered with varnish. The two women wear long white dresses, held up by a strap over the left shoulder. They have yellowish brown skins, darkened somewhat by the varnish which was originally applied to brighten the paint. The heavy locks of hair hanging on their shoulders are black, and from under the broad mass of hair behind hangs the counterpoise of a necklace, a simple black tassel ending in a roundel.

The man who heads the little procession carries over his left shoulder an enormous *ḥes* vase, painted brown and varnished, perhaps to show that it was made of copper. In his right hand he carries a censer with a light yellow, unvarnished handle and a red bowl, varnished to imitate shiny metal, and flecked inside with black representing incense. Curiously enough, the hand at the end of the censer is clenched, perhaps about an invisible handle by which the incense bowl is held. The second man has a pile of linen sheets on his head, all neatly stacked so that the folded sides are on the left. There is a big white sheet on the bottom, with two smaller ones above it; then comes a sheet dyed light yellow; and above that are a white, a red, and lastly another white sheet. Behind this man comes a woman carrying in her right hand a large brown spotted goose, while her left hand is raised to steady a big basket on top of her head. In the basket there are two large stoppered jars like those carried by the big offering bearer girl (K), and six conical loaves of bread. The basket is painted light yellow with black edges and crossbars, but the bottom lines on the sides do not go all the way across. The wine jars are painted red with white stoppers decorated with black spirals, and the loaves of bread are yellow. The second woman, bringing up the rear of the procession, holds a large white goose, the bill and eyes of which are varnished. She carries on her head a basket exactly like her companion's, filled with square white loaves flecked with black.

There are similar groups of offering bearers in different museums, but we need mention only the fine model from el Bersheh in the Museum of Fine Arts, Boston.[3]

1. Such costumes as these make us think of the tale of King Sneferu and the girls who paddled him around his pleasure lake, only those girls had done away with linen dresses and only wore the bead nets. (See A. Erman and A. M. Blackman, *The Literature of the Ancient Egyptians*, p. 39.) Similar beadwork garments were apparently common in ancient Egypt, worn over dresses of white linen, against which they showed excellently well.

2. See above, p. 27.

3. See William Stevenson Smith, *Ancient Egypt as Represented in the Museum of Fine Arts* (Boston), 1942, p. 85, fig. 53.

I V

THE MODELS
OF MEKET-RĒʿʾS BOATS

1. THE TRAVELING BOAT. MODELS N–Q.

On his inspection trips up and down the Nile Meket-Rēʿ went on a traveling boat which was represented in his tomb by four models, two of them showing it under sail as it went up stream before the prevailing north wind of Egypt, and two showing it with the mast and sail lowered and the crew rowing down stream into the breeze (Plates 33–37, 70, 72–74). The four models are the work of two different groups of artisans, one making the feet of the crew out of gesso and giving each man a thick mop of hair, while the other carved the feet out of the same wood as the legs and made the heads smooth shaven. The figures have one thing in common, however: they are made at a larger scale than the boats themselves. If we assume that the men average about one-eighth of their actual size,[1] even the largest boat would be too small for its crew. Taking the hull only, the vessel would be about 12.50 meters long and

45

3.30 meters broad on deck, at a scale of 1:10, and about 3 meters longer and not quite 1 meter wider, if the model was at a scale of 2:25. Such proportions would give the real dahabiyeh of Meket-Rē a length of between 25 and 30 cubits and a beam of 6 or 8 cubits, as the Egyptian himself would measure it, and a ship of this size would have met all his needs when he went traveling up and down river.[2]

The draft of the traveling boat is open to question. No water line is indicated on the hulls of any of these models, and the underwater profile is not reliable, since the Eleventh Dynasty model maker carved the hull deeper than that of an actual boat and made the bottom flat, so that the model would stand securely. The most likely method of estimating the position of the water line is to consider that when the deck planks were taken up for rowing, the oarsmen's feet were about on the water line, standing perhaps on an assumed second deck or on a series of cross timbers. This method of timbering would give an amidships freeboard of about 50 or 60 centimeters above the water, which was probably about what was practical for the ancient Egyptian oarsman. It is possible to consider that the real ship's sides were higher, with the bow and stern decks starting just over the points where the hull broke the water. In one of the models (N) this would give a freeboard of from 85 to 110 centimeters amidships where the vessel was lowest, and as much as 110 to 140 centimeters in the bow. This elevation above the water would make it impossible to work the oars unless those in the bow were far longer than those amidships, but since this was probably not the case and so high a freeboard was unlikely, the lower freeboard is probably nearer the truth. The assumption is, therefore, that the ancient Egyptian vessel was much shallower than these models would indicate from their outside profiles, and that the rowers' feet were practically on the bottom of the vessel.[3]

On the dahabiyeh of Meket-Rē almost all the forecastle was out of water, with its deck tilting up very slightly as it went forward (Plates 70, 72–74). The space below deck was clearly too low for anything except rope or other not too bulky objects, with the result that no weight would be stowed there which would bring the bow of the vessel down.

46

The forecastle was merely the place for the lookout and a landing stage when the ship was run up on the bank. In the ordinary course of events its deck planks would never need to be lifted. The main framework of the vessel, painted red, from which the bow was to all intents and purposes suspended, shows clearly between the four white deck planks. It consists of a central beam with two cross ribs, the wider after rib being the tread of a step going down into the waist of the vessel; around the edge is a gunwale lashed in the bow with black tarred rope, indicated by black paint. In addition to being a landing stage, the bow supported a timber fastened to the longitudinal deck beam which served as a fender. This timber grew thicker toward the bow, over which it curled ingeniously to prevent splintering of the deck if the bow struck against anything, and it was lashed with black tarred rope to the central deck beam just aft of the bow itself and again just aft of the first cross timber of the forecastle. Then, on each model except one (P) where its omission must be accidental, a black spot on either side of the fender doubtless represents the hole through which the mooring or tow rope was passed.

The gunwale continued from forecastle to stern, but aft of the second cross timber in the bow the main deck dropped down one step. Then came ten cross timbers—on Boat O the maker has indicated eleven—on either side of the longitudinal beam which gave the vessel its greatest stiffness and from which the bow and stern were hung. This beam served the purpose of a keel on the under side of the hull, for the ancient Egyptian shipbuilder had not yet invented the keel. Between the timbers of this framework the white pine deck planking was probably movable, and on two of the models (O and Q) some of the planks had been removed to give the rowers a chance to stand on a lower level when they began their rowing stroke and to sit on the cross timbers at the end of each stroke. On three of the models (N–P) an obviously movable cabin occupies most of the deck from side to side of the vessel between the last five timbers. Forward of the cabin on Boat O, being rowed, the planks were taken up between the next seven timbers on each side next the gunwale, the center of the deck, however, being covered. Boat Q has a very small cabin which has been moved from the stern amidships, leaving space for

47

rowers on either side of it the full length of the ship from the forecastle to the poop deck. In this way it was possible to put eighteen men at the oars instead of only twelve as on Boat O, and it would seem likely that if desirable, such an arrangement could always be made when the ship had a small cabin aboard and extra oarsmen were needed. When the deck planks were removed there would be about a meter between the cross beams, or thwarts, which would be ample space for a good rowing stroke. Each rower would start standing with his leg which was next the gunwale raised and his foot on the thwart astern of him and then give a long, slow heave on the sweep which would end with him sitting on the thwart forward of where he had been standing. Everyone who has been on the Nile knows the long, slow stroke still used by the river boatmen.

The poop deck was a step above the main deck, like the forecastle. The last cross timber of the main deck and the very broad cross timber of the poop, which came right against it, were bored through to make a stepping for the tall rudder post. Aft of the last stern cross timber came a broad pine deck plank, tilting up slightly toward the stern of the vessel and covering a small space where something might be stowed, if the hold was crowded. The planking on the outside of the stern rose very sharply at this point, until it was almost vertical all around the after part of the ship, forming a rest for the gigantic steering oar. Inside this planking an additional longitudinal brace, lashed to the inner surface of the hull in two places, was provided for the after part of the vessel to give it greater stiffness. Had this rib gone the length of the ship, it could easily have become a keel, but it seems only to have existed in this high part of the stern.

The ship's rudder post, apparently of oak or some other hard wood, was from 3.50 to 4.40 meters high, depending on what we assume the scale of these models to be (Plate 84). In any case, it must have been tall enough for the steersman to move freely from side to side of the vessel under the rudder shaft when the ship was under way, in order to see around the cabin which was just in front of him. Since this post is always set amidships, directly forward of the rudder rest in the high stern rail, the rudder oar had a slight tendency to throw the bow off its straight course, and that tendency in these models is invariably to port. The base of the post, where it entered the deck, was square in section, but for the greater part of its height the four corner edges were cut away, and at the top they were rounded and slightly grooved. On the port side near the top of the rudder post, a cow's horn was let into it, and the lashing of black tarred rope at the end of the steering oar was passed several times through this horn. The horn stopped the rope from running down the post and the blade of the oar from floating clear of the water and thus being powerless to turn the boat on its course.

The great single rudder oar was two-thirds as long as the whole hull of the ship itself, for it measured some 8 or 10 meters from one end to the other. It was of the same hard wood as the post from which it was hung—probably imported oak. The shaft, or stem, rested in a slight hollow carved in the high timbers of the stern, where it was held by one lashing, and against the top of the rudder post with another lashing, so that the blade, trailing aft, was partly submerged. It could be rotated by a long tiller which pierced its shaft below the upper lashing. Since this tiller was long enough to just clear the deck, the steersman could either stand beside it, or he could squat on the deck and look along either side of the cabin to see how the boat was headed.

The three ropes by means of which the great steering oar of the ship was handled were made especially for these models. This is obvious because their ends—particularly the looped ends of the black cords which hold the rudders—are so often neatly finished off. At the top of the rudder oar there was the black tarred lashing which held the end of the shaft against the post, where the horn prevented it from rising or falling. Across the shaft where it rested in the stern socket another lashing held the blade down in the water. In its simplest form this lashing was merely a stout rope tied over the rounded shaft through two loops of tarred cord passing through holes on either side of the after rest. In a more advanced form this lashing was a loop of white linen rope made fast on the left through the black loop, and on the right, held by an oak wood pin which was permanently tied to the other tarred loop. When the pin was withdrawn the untarred loop would naturally be freed by the rising oar.

49

Finally, there was a preventer line hitched twice around the rudder shaft and made fast to a loop in the deck. When the vessel was securely moored to the bank, the pin was withdrawn from the stern lashing, and the rudder blade popped up out of the water. The tiller was then pulled out and the top rope cast off, after which the preventer line was pulled in and the rudder was stowed on board the vessel until it was to be set in its rest once more.

Immediately aft of the third cross timber on the main deck was the mast stepping (Plates 70, 72–74). It consisted of three oak knees, of which the central one, practically straight-angled, was pegged fast to the main central beam of the deck, while the two side ones had horizontal members bent slightly forward so that their ends could be pegged to the third cross timber. The longitudinal deck beam of the ship was interrupted aft of this point in the spaces between three cross timbers, and its structural function was taken over by two lighter beams running lengthwise of the deck and separated by a space a little greater than the thickness of the mast. Between these beams was a narrow deck plank. It is probably due to an error that on two of the models (N and P) the cross timber in the middle is painted as going right across this plank, for on the other two models (O and Q) it stops at the two narrow fore and aft beams. Perhaps a small block of wood may have been dropped into the slot to continue the interrupted cross timber when the vessel was under sail, to give the ship a bit more rigidity. The nature of the mast stepping below the deck on the bottom of the ship is not known, of course, since the model hull is a solid block of wood. The butt end of the mast on a real vessel must have rested on the bottom of the hull, supported by blocks.

Whenever the breeze favored, the mast was set up and the sail was bent on the spars (Plates 33, 34, 36). Luckily, on one of the models under sail (N) everything was fairly well preserved and still in place, but in all other cases of boats sailing, the rigging had been wrenched away, leaving nothing except the ends of a few cords which, however, are perfectly consistent with the one complete sailing vessel we did find. Obviously this destruction took place before the funeral because so much of the rigging was missing entirely. Even on Yachts T and V where some rigging did exist, both masts were broken, one being burnt and the other one having a section lost, and there was only an incomplete lot of spars left.[4]

When the sail was to be set, the first thing was to cast off any ropes holding the mast and spars in place in the mast crotch, as shown on Boat Q, and then to lift the crotch out of the mast stepping, in order to make way for the foot of the mast itself (Plates 33, 34, 70). The crotch, when not in use, lay on the deck forward. In hauling the mast up, most of the work was done with the heavy forestay, made of alternating black and white ropes for strength and pliability. One end of this was tied to a ring in the top of the copper masthead and the other end eventually made fast to the bow fender. The mast was secured aft, as shown on Boat N, by a white untarred rope tied through the same ring at the masthead and made fast to the rudder post, and on Boat P by from seven to ten black tarred backstays made fast, perhaps permanently, to the rudder post on that vessel. Four men, who stand in the bow of Boat P, and the lookout were doubtless able to haul the mast up, while four other members of the crew, and perhaps the steersman, guided it with the stay ropes. When the mast was erect its foot was probably bound or locked in place in the same way as on Yachts T and V.[5]

To hold the mast up there were also three pairs of double untarred shrouds or stays passing through rings attached to three copper hoops on the upper part of the mast (Plates 34, 70, 71, 84). The topmost of these stays went aft to two men who would eventually make them fast to two cleats on the poop rail, invariably represented by two daubs of black paint. The middle pair of shrouds went to two men who would pass them through cleats on the ship's rail abreast of the cabin. These cleats are shown as being bound with black tarred ropes which not only secure them to the rail of the vessel but give the cleat itself a roughness which helps to prevent the shrouds from slipping. The lowest pair of shrouds usually hung loose and were not attached to the rail, although on Boat N they are provisionally tied through holes bored under the rail, opposite the mast, merely to hold the mast in place. On a real boat going up the Nile, whenever the breeze swung around 20 degrees or more toward the ship's beam, the windward of these two shrouds was made fast in the windward cleat to give the mast more stiffness.

The spars now had to be set. The boom was fastened to the mast with a simple cross lashing, and it was hung in place on twenty-six diagonal ropes, each one of which was permanently bound around one yardarm, carried up and looped about a tie over a hoop of papyrus on the upper part of the mast, and then brought down and bound to the other yardarm (Plates 34, 71). This great number of ropes was obviously needed to support the very long, slender boom at as many points as possible, to prevent it from swinging from side to side when the vessel rolled. Add to them the six double stays, passing through rings on the hoops on the mast at intervals among the boom slings, and there is a veritable forest of ropes on the upper part of the mast. The tip of the mast was sheathed in a copper masthead, with a copper ring attached to the top for the fastening of the fore and back stays, and another ring in front through which to pass the eight halyards holding the upper yard. A rope from each end of the boom, where the foot of the sail was made fast, served as a sheet which was tied around the rudder post on Boat N. Apparently there were no sheet ropes from the upper yard.

The sail was a rectangular piece of stout linen cloth almost twice as wide as it was high, with a leech and bolt rope, made of twisted heavy black and white strands, sewed around the edges (Plates 34, 38, 71). At the four corners a tack rope was attached, which was wound around the ends of the two spars and finished off with a hitch, spreading the sail out. Across the head and foot of the sail a second rope, somewhat lighter than the bolt rope and made of white strands only, was knotted at the four corners of the sail and laced through the tack rope at intervals. At the top of the sail this line was bound to the yard by another rope, which was wrapped around it twice in each interval, and in addition, the halyards were knotted around this rope, perhaps by an error on the part of the model maker, for this means that the halyards had to be cast off every time the sail was unbent. Today the foot of the sail on Boat N is made fast to the boom at its corners only, leaving the light rope through which the lace line at the top passes functionless. It would seem that the lace line at the bottom was omitted by error, or that it was broken and we did not recognize the fragments among the innumerable bits of cordage.

Five members of the crew are shown pulling on the eight halyards which pass through the ring on the masthead (Plates 33, 34, 36, 70, 71). The lack of pulleys with revolving sheaves and the friction of these ropes one on another obviously made the raising of such a large sheet of canvas an arduous task. It must have been possible, however, and once the sail was up, the crew had only to make the halyards fast. This action is not shown on the two traveling boat models, but those of the yacht show that there was a loop of black tarred rope provided for the purpose in the deck beside the mast stepping.[6] To trim the sail, there were two sheet ropes, tied to the ends of the boom, and they are shown on the models as made fast to the rudder post. If the wind varied from dead astern, the boom was hauled around with these ropes, and the bottom shroud, on the side of the ship from which the breeze came, was set to take up some of the strain on that side, as we have already noted; but if it veered more and more broadside to the vessel's course, the round bottom and lack of keel would allow too much leeway to be made, and the sail had to be lowered and the oars got out, to avoid running aground.

When the ship was being rowed down river into the wind the rigging was stowed so as not to interfere with the oarsmen (Plates 37, 72, 74). Loosing the central tie of the lower yard permitted it, with the upper yard, to be swung parallel to the mast. This was then removed from its stepping, and the crotch was set in its place. The mast with its two spars was laid in it, with the butt end of the mast toward the bow and its head aft. The crotch was almost as high as a man and was apparently made of pine, as it is invariably painted white. While we found one such crotch in place on Kitchen Tender S, no spars and mast were resting in it, but they obviously had been so placed. Since they would have rolled off the rounded cabin roof and got in the way of the steersman, they must have been laid in the shallow groove on top of the rudder post, where they could be lashed in place, as we put them on Traveling Boat Q on Plate 37. The sail had already been unlaced from the spars, for on that

53

model we found it folded up and laid on deck aft, but it is fair to suppose that it would have been stowed below deck on a real ship.

The oars used on the traveling boat had spoon blades which were painted white, the handles being red. When found, the oars were invariably slipped into the loops of rope which served as rowlocks, as they would have been when the ship was under sail, to prevent their being broken or lost when the models were being carried to the tomb, but on Plates 37 and 72 they are shown as they would have been when the boat was being rowed. The tops of the handles were whittled to fit into the hands of the rowers.

The cabin of the traveling boat was probably a light, movable shelter, usually set up over the after part of the main deck but occasionally, as in one model (Q), moved forward to a point just aft of the mast stepping and facing aft instead of forward (Plates 33, 35–39, 70, 72–74). On these models the cabin varies from a simple shelter open in front and walled all the way across behind, to a more complicated structure which was probably closer to reality, the differences probably being due to the idiosyncrasies of the makers of the models, since each type of cabin is fairly consistent on the two types of models. In its simplest form the sides of the round-topped cabin are shown as covered with varicolored rugs, like curtains, and the end wall is painted white to represent linen canvas; the two most elaborate cabins are decorated in addition with bull's hide shields, hanging in pairs on either side.

The two most complete models, Boats N and Q, show that in reality the structure of the cabin was about as follows (Plates 38, 39, 84). The framework was of wood, covered inside with white linen canvas. There was a door in the back wall, just to starboard of the rudder post on the axis of the ship, and another door in the middle of a partition which closed the sleeping quarters off from a little porch in front. In every case an actual wooden door was hung in the doorway, hinged in a loop of rope above and in a wooden socket which was attached to the doorsill below, so that when the cabin was moved the door went with it. The shallow porch at the front of the cabin was just deep enough to shelter a chair. The inside room had a barred window on each side, which could be

54

closed by the rugs covering the cabin roof. The cabin on Boat **O** has the rugs rolled up to let the breeze blow through to cool it off. Inside the cabin on Boat **N** there is a bed with legs like those of the deck chair, turned inward and resting on knobs. Under this bunk there are stowed two little traveling trunks with vaulted lids, painted brown to imitate leather. In the cabin of Boat **Q** the trunk is a simple wooden box, painted white.

These models of the dahabiyeh of Meket-Rē' are all brightly colored, from the glistening red copper masthead to the yellow hull of the vessel (Plates 33–39). The colors are unquestionably those of the real ship, but since the models were never intended to be put into water, the paint on them did not have to resist dampness, and simple water colors were therefore sufficient.[7] The outside of the entire hull was painted with yellow ochre up to the rail. The interior of the hull and the gunwale were given a coat of red ochre, as were the deck beams, the rudder post, the steering oar, and the bow bumper. The deck planks were presumably of imported pine or some similar wood, for they are invariably painted white. The cabin was a brightly colored structure with its top covered over with green and yellow linen rugs, except for the back which was of plain white linen canvas, or canvas fastened to the red wooden framework in which the red door was hung. The shields hanging on the sides of the cabin were of spotted black and white or red bulls' hides, with the hair left on them. The cordage was natural white linen, except such fixed stays and lashings as needed extra strength and did not have to be pliable, and those were all black to represent tarring. The mast was painted yellow, and its head and three shroud hoops were of copper; the spars were yellow with black stripes; and the mast had a complicated pattern of white papyrus lashings and black ropes crisscrossing to support the white linen sail.

To man this vessel a crew of from fifteen to twenty-one is shown upon its deck (Plates 33–37). First there is the captain, who is always shaven headed, since he is of the effendi class, and this is true even on Boats **N** and **O** where all the rest of the crew have thick mops of black hair. He wears a long white skirt from his waist to his ankles, because he was never supposed to do any heavy work, and on Boat **N** he carries a staff of office. On the other three models he stands on deck facing Meket-Rēʿ with his arms humbly crossed over his breast, awaiting the orders of the great man. Next in rank are the steersman, who stands or sits beside the tiller, and the lookout, who stands in the bow, holding a bumper covered with spotted bull's hide in his right hand and pointing out the course with his left. Both helmsman and bowman on Boats N and O have bushy hair, showing that they are only members of the crew. On both models of the ship under sail the four men who have just hauled on the forestay and made it fast to the bow stand just aft of the forecastle, with no further duties for the present; five others pull on the halyards beside the mast; and four more squat on the deck holding shrouds and back stays, ready to belay them to the cleats on the gunwale beside the cabin and abreast of the step up to the poop. The crew, including the captain, thus consists of sixteen men on the two vessels making sail. On Boat O, where the crew has the oars out, there are twelve men rowing, who, with the captain, lookout and steersman, make fifteen in the ship's company, while on Boat Q there are eighteen men rowing, who, with the three others, make a total of twenty-one.

On all four traveling boats Meket-Rēʿ himself, clad in a long white garment draped over one or both shoulders, is seated on a stool or on a low-bottomed, high-backed chair (Plates 38, 39). He is smelling a lotus bud or a partly opened lotus flower, and listening to his musicians or giving orders to the captain, who stands before him. Usually he is in the cool shade of the cabin porch, but on Boat Q where the crew of eighteen oarsmen is tugging away at the oars as the vessel heads into the wind, he has ordered the movable cabin to be turned around so that its open end faces aft out of the wind, while he has had his stool moved up on the forecastle deck. There he sits to windward of the crew. On this boat and on the large vessel sailing up stream (N) a steward sits inside the cabin, keeping a watchful eye on the master's luggage and handy to his call.

To beguile the tedium of long hours of river travel, a singer, seated on the deck beside Meket-Rēʿ's chair, is shown on Boats N and O, and on the latter ship a harpist accompanies him (Plates 38, 39, 77). The singer pats his lips to give his voice a warbling note, still much affected by soloists along the Nile. The harpist is blind but, as is so often the case in Egypt today, that disability does not prevent his accompanying the singer on his instrument. With someone to lead him around, a blind musician was not so badly off. The musician's harp is in front of him, sitting in its special wooden rest on the deck. This rest, painted red, has a crosspiece mitered near the back to make it sit squarely, a block in front with a socket in it to hold the foot of the harp, and a slightly curved and hollowed-out cradle in which the instrument stands. The harp itself is painted yellow, and its sounding box is painted to represent a covering of black and white spotted bull's hide. Its white wooden bridge is pierced for seven strings, and there are seven alternating black and yellow pegs let into the end of the curved neck. Originally the harp had real gut strings.

2. THE KITCHEN TENDER. MODELS R, S.

Meket-Rē''s river travels were evidently such that a kitchen boat had to accompany his dahabiyeh in order to provide food and drink for him and his companions (Plates 40–44, 75, 76). Two models of such a tender were found in the *sirdāb* of his tomb (R, S). Since the traveling boat was not very large, cooking meals on board would have been a nuisance to the great man, and therefore the kitchen boat followed behind and was moored alongside at meal times. As in the case of the traveling boats, the two models probably represent only a single real boat, in one case (R) sailing and in the other (S) being rowed, but the activities vary on the two models. On Boat R, now in Cairo, jars of beer and wine standing in a rack, joints of meat hanging on ropes strung between two posts, and two baskets, probably assumed to be filled with bread, are all stowed inside the cabin, while forward on deck near the mast stepping there are a large jar with domed stopper, presumably full of fermenting beer, and a brazier for cooking. On Tender S, now in New York, flour is being ground, dough mixed and shaped into loaves and cakes, and the bread baked. On shipboard, as on shore, the tasks of baking and brewing went hand in hand.

57

The construction of the kitchen tender was exactly like that of the traveling boat, described above, and both models are obviously the work of the same makers (Plates 75, 76, 84). The cabin on Tender R is decorated with two bull's hide shields on each side; on Boat S the cabin is undecorated and is closed at the back. The small post in front of the cabin on the former boat was specially erected so that the ends of the ropes on which the cuts of meat were hung could be attached to it; the other ends of the ropes were made fast to the rudder post at the rear of the cabin.

The personnel of the crew on the kitchen tender was the same as on the traveling boat, fourteen men being needed when the boat was under sail, and only ten when it was being rowed, of which the lookout and the helmsman were two in each case (Plates 40–44, 86). All the men in the crew, as well as the menservants, are painted dark red and have smooth-shaven heads. The crew on Tender R is in the act of hoisting the sail, but this and its mast and spars were missing when the model was found by us. The mast crotch was lying on deck forward. The ropes from the sail still remained in the hands of the men, showing that the boat was fully rigged when the model was made. The lookout holds in his right hand a black and white spotted bumper such as we have already seen in use on the traveling boat. A mooring peg was found on the deck. Fewer oarsmen were apparently needed on the kitchen boat, only four on each side being shown on Tender S, but this may be because there was not room enough for more, since the hull is shorter, even though wider, than that of the traveling boat. The men are seated on the thwarts as they row and not standing as on the traveling boats. In the photograph of the traveling boat with its kitchen tender now in the Metropolitan Museum (Plate 43), the oars have been removed from the rowers' hands on the kitchen boat and have been slipped in the oarlock loops lengthwise along the gunwale, as they would have been when the vessel was under sail. It was in this position that we found them, for they had been so placed for convenience and safety in carrying the model to the tomb.

In addition to the crew there is one manservant at work on Tender R (Plates 40, 41, 44, 77). He is seated on the forward deck, beside a four-legged brazier on which a bowl of stew or pudding is cooking. In his right hand he holds a fan to blow up the fire in the brazier. The servants at work on Tender S consist of two women grinding flour, four men mixing dough and shaping it into loaves and cakes, and one man tending a baking oven. The hand mill in front of each of the women is single and not double like the heavier ones in the bakery and brewery model already described, and it is set on broad feet front and back instead of having a solid pedestal, since it needed to be light and easy to move for use on board ship. The mills are painted yellow and the millstones the women are using are left in the natural color of the wood, to represent gritstone. Like the women in the bakery model, these servants wear white shifts, with a strap over the left shoulder, and have their hair drawn back over both shoulders to keep it out of the way. Behind the two women is a rectangular tray like the one in the brewery, probably for the dough containing the yeast left over from the last batch, and it also is set up on four feet so that it can be moved easily. Near these women is one of the men mixing dough in a vat, and in the center of the deck near the mast crotch is the oven with a man tending it. Inside the cabin are three other men, one of whom is standing in a red vat mixing the mash with his feet, while at the same time he is shaping dough into loaves on a round white slab set on top of a similar red vat. A second man makes lumps of dough into cakes on a sloping rectangular board before which he is seated. Beside him are two barrels, probably containing flour or perhaps already-mixed dough. The third man stands before a vat on top of which is a tray of cakes he is arranging for the baker. The baking oven is a tall square stove like two in the bakery model except that it is set up on feet. It is painted black with streaks of red on top to show that it is hot. The baker, fan in hand, is seated before the fire hole in the front of the oven, on top of which is a black pot with a lid.

3. THE YACHT. MODELS T–W.

It is hard to say whether the makers of the four boats T–W (Plates 45–50) thought of them as models of an actual yacht in which Meket-Rē took his ease in the cool of the evening on the river, or of a funerary barque for the voyage of the dead man to and from Abydos. Perhaps their makers were not very clear on this point themselves.

On all four boats a figure of Meket-Rē' sits enthroned on a primitive, blocklike chair which probably had not been used in actual life for countless ages, as if his dead spirit were thought of (see Plate 1). But on two boats (T, U) he is accompanied by his son, In-yotef, who is seated on the deck beside him with one leg under him and the other knee up, an attitude which would not be adopted if the son were sitting beside a funerary statue of his father. The carving of these four little figures is the work of a real sculptor, who lavished great care on them, and they are more statuesque perhaps than the figures of Meket-Rē' on the traveling boats. In front of Meket-Rē' on one of the models (T) there stand three offering bearers or priests, shaven-headed and wearing long white skirts, who hold respectively a censer, a ceremonial leg of beef, and a papyrus scroll on which is inscribed in black ink, "a thousand of bread and beer, a thousand of beef and fowl." On all four boats there is also a large *hes* vase, in two cases (T, U) bearing Meket-Rē''s name. These details suggest a funerary ceremony, but since Meket-Rē' and In-yotef are similarly represented on the Sporting Boat (X), which can in no sense be thought of as a funerary barque, the idea that these models were to be buried with their deceased owner must have influenced the makers in their representation of him. Personally I am inclined to consider the figures of Meket-Rē' as those of the living man and their likeness to tomb statues as an idiosyncrasy of the makers, and therefore I shall refer to these boats as yachts and not as funerary barques.

The hull of the yacht is lighter and narrower than that of the traveling boat. The four models average 132 centimeters in length, but they have a beam amidships of only 28.5 centimeters and narrow rapidly both fore and aft (Plates 78–81). We have no accurate data on which to base an idea of how much freeboard there was on a real yacht, but it was probably very little. Here the boat was propelled by men who squatted on the deck and held their paddles upright, so that less freeboard was necessary than on the traveling boat. That the yacht sat very low in the water is more than likely, for it had a half-round splash rail running the length of the waist of the vessel. The hull on the models is painted light green, ornamented along the gunwale with a band of stripes of various colors—blue, white and yellow, or yellow, red, white and black in different combinations.

The striking difference, however, between the hulls of the yacht and of the traveling boat was in the bow and stern (Plates 78–81, 84, 85). Both bow and stern were exaggeratedly long and roughly cylindrical, the bow-piece turning up almost vertically and the stern-piece curving forward and then up, and they terminated in large knobs, or buttons, obviously imitating conventionalized ends of bound papyrus stalks cut off just above a tie. This is typical of a class of vessel usually connected with funerary barques, the form of which was carried over from the primitive papyrus raft into boats of wood.[8] Prow and stern are painted yellowish brown, in two cases with blue zigzag and in two with black crisscross lines on broad white bands on either side, representing formalized stitching. Obviously the model is decorated to simulate a bow and stern sheathed in some sort of fabric, possibly leather, laced tightly in place. A band of colored stripes indicates the tie at the base of the knob.

The main deck was not sunk below the bow and stern as on the traveling boat, but otherwise it was constructed in the same way, with beams painted red and the deck planks white (Plates 78–81). Since the paddler did not have to tug on the shaft of a long, almost horizontal oar and could squat on deck, the deck planks are all in place on these model yachts, but they are represented as being movable.

The steering gear of the yachts was doubled by having a rudder oar on both sides of the high stern post, which because of its shape prevented a single rudder from being installed on the ship's axis, as on the traveling boat (Plates 78–81). The next to the last cross timber—or the second from the last, as it is represented on two of the models—was apparently thicker and stronger than the rest, and close to its outer ends two sturdy rudder posts were erected. On two boats (V, W) the top of each post was decorated with a hawk's head. To these posts the upper ends of the rudder oars were lashed. The stern narrowed to almost nothing, and above its last cross timber a beam was attached, half round in section and long enough to overhang the water on either side of the stern, thus providing a firm rest for the two steering oars. The oars were lashed to this rudder rest with ropes which passed through loops of tarred rope let into the rest on either side of each oar. Preventer lines to counteract the drag on the rudders were tied to loops of tarred rope let into the deck (T, U) or into the ends of the rudder rest (V, W). The lashing of the upper ends of the rudder oars to the posts was of the simplest, the oars being longer than those on the traveling boat and the tillers set forward of the posts, thus stopping the rudders from drifting free of the lashing, if the preventer lines went adrift.

The models of Meket-Rē''s yacht, like the traveling boats and kitchen tenders, show it being sailed up river before the following breeze (T, V) and being paddled down stream (U, W) (Plates 45, 78, 85). When they were sailing there was very little difference in the simple rigging of the two classes of vessel—the yacht and the traveling boat. Models T and V were fully rigged when they were made, and on Plate 45 Yacht T is shown with the rigging replaced as far as possible, considering the condition in which we found it.[9] The forestays were made fast around the top of the prow, and the halyards were tied through heavy loops of tarred rope let into the deck aft of the mast stepping. On Yacht T a similar loop of tarred rope let into the forward deck doubtless was used to make fast a mooring rope, thus serving the same purpose as the hole in the bow fender of the traveling boat. On one yacht (T) a loop of tarred rope was tied through holes on either side of the mast stepping, and when the mast was set in place a wooden pin was slipped through these two loops, effectively holding the mast in the stepping; and on the other (V) a stout rope was wound round and round the upright part of the mast stepping to hold the mast in place. Bits of shrouds and backstays of thin tarred cordage existed on Yacht V, tied through holes in the rails and in the rudder rest on the after deck.

There was no real cabin on the yacht, a simple canopy to shade the owner from the blazing rays of the sun being all the shelter needed on such a pleasure boat (Plates 45–49). The construction of the canopy was that of an ancient type of shrine or baldachin, and a form of it appeared on all funerary barques. The light roof, arching up from a cavetto cornice across the front, was supported by four tent-pole columns, the shafts of which were decorated with blue and yellow horizontal bands. The open sides allowed the cool river breezes to pass across the deck. Because the deck sloped forward slightly under the canopy, a wedge-shaped platform, painted white, was put under Meket-Rēʿs chair, to make a level place on which it could sit.

In addition to Meket-Rēʿ, In-yotef, and the offering bearers already referred to, there are on Yacht T five officers, whose skins seem to be painted the same dark color as the crew but who are distinguished by their longer white kilts. Two of these men hold scepters in their right hands, and their left arms hang at their sides; two others are in a more subservient attitude with both arms crossed on the chest; and still another has the left arm only so crossed and holds a scepter in his right hand. The crew of this yacht consists of thirteen men, nine of whom are in the act of hoisting the sail, which is now missing (Plates 45, 47, 50). In the stern are the two steersmen, standing beside the tillers on the rudders; on the forward deck there is a man holding a hide-covered bumper and another man with a punting pole, who leans forward pushing the boat off. On the deck near these last two lie another punting pole, a mast crotch, two mooring pegs and the mallet for driving them in, and a gangplank. The other model of the yacht sailing (V) has only one officer apparently, and he stands before Meket-Rēʿ with both arms crossed on his chest. Three men on the forward deck may be officers but are more likely additional members of the crew. The latter consists of eight men hoisting sail, now missing, and the two steersmen.

On the two models of the yacht being paddled (U, W) there are five officers on Yacht U and probably only two on Yacht W (Plates 46, 48, 86). The man on the forward deck may have held a scepter, but it is more likely that he is the lookout, who held in his right hand a bumper, now missing, as on Yacht T. The crew on these yachts consists of sixteen paddlers, eight on each side, and the two steersmen at the rudder oars. The paddles are painted black, with yellow bands just above their flat, pointed blades.[10]

63

On each of the yachts there stands on deck in front of Meket-Rē' a large *ḥes* vase, painted yellow with white bands, those up the side decorated with black zigzag lines representing stitching (Plates 50, 77). On Yachts T and U the vases are inscribed around the shoulder, below the white band, with a horizontal line of hieroglyphs containing the name of Meket-Rē', confirming his ownership of the boats. The inscription is an offering formula:

"A boon given by the king (and by) Osiris, Lord of Busiris; an invocation-offering (consisting of) bread, beer, beef, and fowl, for the one in honor, the Hereditary Prince, Meket-Rē'."

4. THE SPORTING BOAT. MODEL X.

Two other boats, to supply Meket-Rē' with fowl and fish through the ages, completed his fleet of vessels, if we may judge from the models found in his tomb. The first of these is a Sporting Boat (X)—a fishing and fowling skiff, which was a modification of the types of boat used for traveling and pleasure (Frontispiece and Plate 51).

The hull of the skiff was fairly long but very narrow and low-sided, and on the model it is painted black outside, with the deck beams red and the planks white (Plates 82, 86). There was no fender attached to the bow as on the traveling boat. The deck amidships, provided with wide rails, was a little below the level of the fore and after decks. The stern was low and open, since the outer planking did not rise abruptly around the afterdeck, as on the traveling boat, and it terminated in a broad, flat-topped knob, similar to that on the yacht. The skiff is shown being paddled, the crew of six men who wield the paddles sitting on deck with one leg under them and one knee raised. The usual mast stepping existed, so the boat could be sailed if desired, but the mast must have been short and light, for the stepping and the slot for the mast were smaller than on the traveling boat. A small mast crotch and a fragment of the mast were found near the model.

64

THE MODELS OF MEKET-RĒ''S BOATS

The steering gear on the sporting boat was a curious combination of the two types we have already discussed. Because of the shape of the stern, the rudder oar could not be mounted as in the traveling boats. Instead of two oars as in the yachts there was only one extending from the longitudinal beam, where it was lashed to a rudder post, to the starboard side just forward of the stern. The rudder presents no new features, but the method of hanging it shows two differences. In the first place, the rudder post was an oblong plank with a square crotch in the top in which the upper end of the rudder oar rested and was lashed, with the tiller forward of the post. The rudder rest on the starboard quarter of the hull was a wooden hook, lashed to the gunwale by two wide ties, which are represented on the model by patches of black paint. The rudder oar was held in place in this hook by a rope wound round and round them and tied to a hole bored in the gunwale just aft of the hook. Apparently no preventer line was needed on the rudder oar. Thus the rudder was permanently set to throw the boat's bow to starboard. To steer the bow to port, the tiller would have to be thrown hard over, and the boat would lose a good deal of headway. Obviously, speed was not possible or required on this type of vessel.

In place of a cabin on the sporting boat there was only a shelter with a rounded top supported on a grille of light wooden poles (Plates 51, 82, 83). The top of the shelter is represented as covered with a colored rug, and on either side of it hangs a black and white spotted bull's hide shield, attached by red crisscross lines indicating stitching. Lashed to each side of the grille below the covering are four black poles for a clap-net in which ducks and other birds were snared. Just below the rounded top of each pole is a groove for the net cord; the bottom end is pointed, to stick into the muddy bottom of the marshes. There were also nine black net pegs, four of them with notched tops to hold the ropes, which were found tied together with cord.

Meket-Rē' and his son sit on deck watching the various activities taking place on the boat (Plates 51, 53). Meket-Rē' himself is seated on a blocklike chair similar to the one on the yacht. In-yotef sits on deck beside his father, with his left knee raised and his right leg under him. Both

Meket-Rēˤ and In-yotef have shaven heads and are painted the light yellow color indicative of members of the leisure class. Their figures are too large in scale to sit under the shelter, but the maker of the model probably intended that they should do so. Perhaps, however, the shelter was supposed to serve only as a place to store the birds which had been caught in the clap-net before it was dismantled and stowed away. Some of the birds are being brought to Meket-Rēˤ by a girl and a man. The girl wears a long white shift, over the shoulders of which is a bead net, painted green, red, and yellow, which is not unlike that on the offering bearer girl described above, but is much shorter. She also wears a broad collar, bracelets, and anklets, made of beads of various colors, and around the top of her head is a white fillet with its ties hanging down behind. In her right hand she carries a mallard duck by its wings. The man accompanying her has been engaged in netting birds for he has a broad white band over his left shoulder to protect it, and in each hand he carries a bunch of coots tied together by their legs. The man standing in the waist of the skiff is an overseer, obviously a member of the effendi class like those shown in the models of Meket-Rēˤ's estate, since he is painted light yellow and has a shaven head.

In addition to the man carrying coots, there are four men who are engaged in harpooning fish and attending to them after they are landed on deck (Plates 51, 53, 83). All these men are represented as dark-skinned from exposure to the sun and have heavy heads of hair. Two men on the forward deck are throwing harpoons, and on their left wrists hang the reels on which the lines from the harpoon points were wound. Two large fish have been caught, one a long red *Mormyrus* which is being carried on the shoulder and outstretched arm of the fisherman standing beside Meket-Rēˤ. The other, a flat white *Tilapia nilotica*, or *bolti*, lies on deck at the feet of a fisherman, who is kneeling down to remove the harpoon point from it. The men all wear short white kilts and have a broad white strap over the left shoulder to protect the skin when hauling on the ropes of the bird net.

The lookout on the forward deck, who holds a forked punting pole, the helmsman at the tiller in the stern, and the six men paddling the skiff, three on each side, constituted the personnel needed for such a boat. Lying on deck at the feet of the lookout is a mooring peg. The paddles in the hands of the men are similar in all respects to those used on the yachts.

5. *A PAIR OF FISHING CANOES. MODEL Y.*

The model of two canoes with a trawl between them (Y) which was found with Meket-Rē''s other boat models was also included to provide food for him. This model obviously represents actual papyrus rafts, made of bundles of papyrus reeds bound together at frequent intervals—the earlier craft made by the Egyptians and especially suited for use in swamps and marshes (Plates 52, 53).[11]

In the model the canoes are painted bright green, with yellow ochre lines indicating the binding of the bundles to each other. The bow and stern curved upward above the last tie, the stern ending in a thick knob and the bow in a similar but much smaller knob, representing the cut-off ends of the reeds. An extra bundle was added on each side to form a round gunwale, and a large bundle, roughly rectangular in shape, was placed inside to make a level deck, marked on the model with longitudinal black lines. To accommodate the trawl net stretched between them, the two model canoes were mounted on a flat board, painted green to represent water. The net, a big pocket, its opening facing in the direction in which the canoes were paddled,[12] was made of white rope with heavy black rope around the edge of the opening and reinforcing the center of the bottom. The upper edge of the net opening was supported by eight floats of unpainted wood on the presumed surface of the water, and the lower edge was held down by seven sinkers, probably of lead or stone since they are painted a dark color. To either side of the opening were tied the heavy ropes which went to the hands of three men on board each of the canoes, who dragged the trawl along as the boat was propelled through the water. Because the net was heavy when full, each of these men wore a wide white band over his left shoulder, to protect his skin when he threw his whole weight into the job of hauling on the rope.

In addition to the three men dragging the net, there is on one of

67

the canoes in the model another fisherman, who also wears a band over his shoulder but is seated on deck, helping to land the fish as they are caught. He holds a fish in his left hand, and two others lie on deck near him. These fish and several others caught in the net can be identified as well-known kinds of Nile fish—the *bolti*, *bynni*, *Mormyrus*, and Nile perch. The fishermen are shown as dark-skinned, with heavy heads of dark hair, and they wear short white skirts.

Each canoe was paddled by two men sitting on deck fore and aft. Except that they have no band over the shoulder, they are just like the fishermen. At the time the photographs shown on Plate 52 were taken, the canoes were by error assembled with the paddlers sitting as though they were rowing, facing the stern instead of the bow, and with their paddles grasped in their hands like oars. This mistake was due to the fact that when the canoes were cleared of the débris on them, the men did face in the wrong direction and must have been turned around on the pegs which held them in place on deck by mistake when they were made. Because of the position of the men, we also turned the trawl around and wrong side up, but it should, of course, face in the direction it is being dragged and not toward the stern, as in the photographs. However, the open end of the trawl was facing forward as it should be when we found the model, as can easily be seen in Plate 5. The paddles are just like the ones already seen in use on the yacht and the sporting boat, painted black with white lashings.

1. See below, p. 76.
2. See R. O. Faulkner, *Journal of Egyptian Archaeology*, vol. 26 (1940), pp. 3–9.
3. Cf. two actual contemporary ships found at Dahshur and now in the Cairo Museum: J. de Morgan, *Fouilles à Dahchour, mars-juin, 1894*, pp. 81–83, pls. XXIX–XXXI; G. A. Reisner, *Models of Ships and Boats* (*Catalogue général des antiquités égyptiennes du Musée du Caire*), 1913, p. 83, no. 4925; p. 85, no. 4926.
4. See below, pp. 98, 100.
5. See above, p. 62.
6. See plates 76 and 84.
7. Possibly the hull of an actual boat had a coating of beeswax applied at least to all parts which were submerged or exposed to the wet, but there is no evidence on this point other than the obvious fact that a boat coated with watercolor

could scarcely have made a single river voyage without ending a very sorry sight. The use of beeswax is suggested because it would not greatly alter the colors of the paint, and it would resist dampness, while the ancient Egyptian varnish, which was merely a water-soluble gum, dissolves when it is wet even today.

8. Reisner, *ibid.*, pp. xvii–xxi. Cf. M.M.A. 14.3.23.

9. See below, p. 98.

10. When the model was found the paddles had been stacked on deck, as shown in Plate 46, for convenience in carrying the model to the tomb, but the ends were whittled to fit into the paddlers' hands, which in some cases were stained with the black paint on the paddles.

11. Reisner, *ibid.*, p. xvii; James Henry Breasted, *Journal of Egyptian Archaeology*, IV (1917), pp. 174 ff. and see also p. 255.

12. See below, p. 102.

V

GENERAL REMARKS
ON THE MODELS

THERE can be no doubt about the purely Theban character of these representations of ancient Egyptian life. Models from the north always have houses and shops painted gray to represent Nile mud plaster, for in the Memphite region there is no desert clay which would serve to cover over mud-brick walls. Theban models like those belonging to Meket-Rē̔ invariably have walls and ground painted with yellow ochre to represent the desert clay called ḥīb by the modern Egyptians. Then, too, the subjects shown in Upper Egyptian models are not always the same as those of the neighborhood of Memphis. This is not so much that the people of Upper and Lower Egypt had different customs as that the model makers of the two regions were in the habit of showing different activities. Thus, carpenter shops found at Sakkāreh usually have a man with an adze making a wooden pillow on a chopping block, or using a bow drill—things never shown in Theban models. Sometimes groups from the North show potters and stone vase makers, but apparently no such trades are to be found in any southern models. On the other hand, it would seem that a residence, such as A and B, or a cattle census, like C, are representations not known in the North. At the time Meket-Rē' was a young man Egypt had been separated into two countries for some eighty years,[1] and it was apparently just at this time that the making of large wooden groups of figures became general.

The color used to paint the skins of the men and women in the various models belonging to Meket-Rē' is typical of what we should expect among the people of Upper Egypt. Men of the higher social classes are usually represented in the models as having light complexions and shaven heads. This is always true of Meket-Rē' himself and his son, when the latter is shown with his father. The same smooth heads and light colored skins are given to offering bearers, scribes, and overseers, to all but one of the butchers, to the cooks and brewers, and to four of the carpenters, all of whom worked in the house. Herdsmen, cattle feeders, a man plucking a goose in the butcher shop, and all carpenters except the four mentioned seem to have led outdoor lives, for they have heavy black hair and all are sunburned and therefore painted a rich, red ochre color. The same convention holds on one pair of boats—one boat under sail (N) and one being rowed (O)—as well as on the Sporting Boat (X) and the Fishing Canoes (Y). Here again, Meket-Rē' and his son, the officers carrying batons, the stewards, and the musicians did not have to expose themselves to the sun and had their hair shaved off for coolness. On these ships, however, all sailors, the fowlers, and the fishermen, who led outdoor lives, have thick black hair as a protection from the hot sun and are dark complexioned. On the other boats—Traveling Boats P and Q, the Kitchen Tenders (R, S), and the four yachts (T–W)—no such distinction is made between those who led sheltered and those who led exposed lives. The men in those models have shaven heads. All women, of course, have long hair and light colored complexions.

The native sycamore-fig tree supplied the wood for those bulkier parts of the models such as the hulls of the boats and the walls of the shop models which required no detailed carving. The latter were constructed of sycamore boards from 2 to 3 centimeters thick, they usually had a cleat underneath each end, and in the better-made ones the corners were mitered. Good joinery was impossible, however, with such soft and coarse-grained timber, and the cracks and joints—some clumsily wide— were filled with plaster and glue (gesso) which was spread smoothly over the whole surface. When a crack developed in the poorly seasoned planks of which the large cattle review model (C) was made, it was hidden under a repair of such gesso, and in the models on which a roof was put after their completion (E, J) painted gesso was used to mask the cracks. The paintbrushes were made of black hairs, a few of which were shed in the paint and are still stuck to the models. Only the two models of the Residence (A, B) were made of better material—a straight-grained, co-niferous wood which was probably a pine or cedar imported from Asia Minor or Syria. In these two models not only was the material better but the joinery was excellent, with mitered corners masked on top in the manner of the best Middle Kingdom boxes and coffins.

Almost all accessories which required a certain amount of detailed carving were also made of the same coniferous wood as models A and B. Exceptions were the bulky bodies of cattle which might be made of syca-more, but if they were, the legs, ears, horns, and tails were of pine. Other exceptions were dictated by a desire for realism. In the Carpenter Shop (J) the plank being ripsawed is pine, but the sawyer's post fixed upright in the court is native acacia, as it very likely was in actuality. For the same reason mooring pegs and mallets on boats might be of native tama-risk (U, W), and mast steppings and steering oars of an imported hard wood, which is probably oak (N–S). Likewise, copper was used for the blades of carpenters' tools (J) and for the fittings on a mast (N). The use of copper to line the tanks in the residence models (A, B) was, of course, not realistic but was due to the desire to make them capable of holding water. The sails of the boats were of linen, and the cords were made espe-cially for the models. The heavy cord in the cabin of Boat O was made by taking a bunch of linen threads about 260 centimeters long, doubling them over in the middle, twisting them together, and knotting them at the end. The same method was employed in making all the lashings of rud-ders, the doubled-over end of each cord providing the necessary loop.

All the figures of men and women were carved out of coniferous

73

wood. Those of Meket-Rē' and his son on Yachts T and U were made by special artists. Those of workmen and sailors were turned out by other makers in quantity, the bodies and legs carved in one piece, and the arms made separately and pegged on, with the joints at the shoulders liberally smeared with gesso. In this fashion a few stock types of bodies could be put to an infinite number of uses. A squatting man could be made into a carpenter, a sailor or a cook according to the arms given him, and a standing man could be a herdsman, a harpooner, or a worker in a granary. Even the arms themselves were whittled out in quantities, and clenched hands were usually drilled through, whether they were to hold anything or not. Two methods were in vogue for the treatment of the feet. Some makers carved them in one piece with the legs, and set pegs under them for fastening the figures in place. This was almost invariably the way the figures of women were made, except for the two big Offering Bearers (K and L), whose left feet are separate pieces of wood.[2] The other method was to have the legs terminate in pegs which were set in holes in the pedestals, the feet being modeled separately in gesso, which was squeezed into place while still soft.

Hair was painted black, shaven heads light red, eyes black and white, and garments white; flesh tones were brown and yellow. Both flesh and hair were varnished with a water-soluble gum, and the colors as they exist today probably vary somewhat depending on the grade of varnish used. The brown of the figures on Boat S, and presumably in all other cases where this color exists, was made by varnishing over a deep yellow ochre. This can be seen on the legs of the man kneading dough in the tub on Boat S, where by an oversight the varnish was omitted and where the color therefore remains unaltered. Yellow was probably obtained by varnishing a very light ochre. This varnish has darkened from exposure to sunlight since the models were unearthed.

Nearly every figure of a man or woman had a bit of linen wrapped around it to represent clothing—an additional touch of unnecessary realism, since all were carved as clothed figures. The only ones without this bit of cloth were the large Offering Bearers (K, L) and the well-carved statuettes of Meket-Rē' and his son on Boats T and U. These bits of linen

74

covered the modeled and painted clothes, being merely wrapped around the waists of men wearing short skirts but covering the whole body of Meket-Rē' and of women in long dresses. Usually the scraps of cloth were square bits torn from sheets, in a few cases wrapped around the figure with the fringed end up at the waist. On Boat X the linen skirts were most carefully done, an extra little strip of cloth being provided for a sash or belt, while the white painted bands over the left shoulders of the fishermen were covered with an actual strip of linen. Insects had eaten holes in most of the pieces of linen, however, and had reduced many to mere shreds. None were restored by us because it was thought more interesting to leave the figures entirely visible, but those pieces of cloth which were in good condition and which remained in place were left so, and in one or two cases were made fast with glue.

It seems likely that one group of artisans whittled out the bodies of the figures, while others constructed boat hulls or buildings. To a certain extent we can recognize the output of several such groups of workmen, and we gather the impression that Meket-Rē' patronized a number of different model makers' shops in preparing his tomb equipment. For example, the two models of the Residence (A, B) are clearly the work of the same hands. The materials and the workmanship are excellent, and the subject so rare that no other examples have survived. The Butcher Shop (E) and the Bakery and Brewery (G) come from another source, and the Granary (F) and Carpenter Shop (J) from a third, both of which did very good work. A cruder group of models comprises the Inspection of Cattle (C) and the Stable (D), the Weaving Shop (H), and the fishing boats (X, Y). The figures of Meket-Rē' and his son in models C and X show a striking similarity. Of traveling boats there were two sets from the hands of two different groups of makers. One was the larger pair of boats (N, O) on which the sailors have thick black hair, and the other, the pair of boats to smaller scale (P, Q) on which everyone has a shaven head. Perhaps the pair of Kitchen Tenders (R, S) belong with these last, since the men have shaven heads. It is possible that the larger set was procured from the shop which produced F and J and that the smaller pair came from the makers of E and G. Likewise, there were two pairs of yachts (T, U and V, W) coming from two different sources. Some of the figures on the second pair of yachts are very suggestive of certain figures in the Inspection of Cattle (C). Furthermore, one should not forget that all these yachts have the figures of the crews as well as those of higher class personages shown with shaven heads. The figures of Meket-Rē' and his son come from other hands than those which fashioned the crews, and those on Yachts T and U, although somewhat hard, wooden, and staring, have a surprising dignity for their size and show a wonderful care in the modeling of even the smallest details. Foreheads, noses, knees, calves, and even the exposed sole of In-yotef's foot are all carved with conscientious exactness. These two yachts at least were made to order, for they bear the name of Meket-Rē' on the vases standing on the decks.

It would hardly have been in character for the ancient Egyptian to feel bound to consistent proportions, and we can scarcely expect to find that the makers of these models adhered to a uniform scale. Figures of men might be as large as one-seventh life size (22–24 centimeters high); they were sometimes a little less than one-eighth (20–21 centimeters); rarely they were one-ninth (19 centimeters); but the helmsmen on the four yachts (T–W) were as small as one-tenth (averaging 17 centimeters). These proportions are based on the assumption that the figures represent men from about 164 to 170 centimeters (5 feet, 4 inches to 5 feet, 6 inches) in stature. Such figures were too large ever to have gone through the doors of the shops in which they stood, and they would have swamped the boats they were on, if the boats were proportionately no larger than they are shown.

In fact, in proportion to the buildings the men are nearly twice too large. If we assume that the details of each building are roughly to the same scale—a condition which is not improbable—we may take as a handy unit of measure the heights of the door openings. The doors should be almost two meters high, and calculating from them we arrive at a scale of about one-fifteenth full size for four of the shops (D, G, H, J). Two others (E, F) are as large as one-twelfth actual size, and the porch from which the cattle are reviewed (C) would appear to be at about the same scale. The two models of the residence (A, B) are obviously at a much smaller scale. If the intercolumnar spaces as well as the doors are considered, the scale of these two models can hardly be larger than one-twentieth and may be less.

For the vessels perhaps the most convincing calculation is one which can be made on the timbering of the decks of the Traveling Boats (N–Q). The assumptions here are that to row in Egyptian fashion the space required for each rower is from 80 to 100 centimeters and that the correct number of thwarts is shown on the models.[2] Based on these assumptions we arrive at a scale somewhere between one-tenth and two-twenty-fifths, which is consistent for their cabins and for the bed inside the cabin on Boat N. Calculations on the yachts are somewhat less certain, but in all probability the scale to which they were made differs little from that of the traveling boats.

Not only did Meket-Rēʿ procure his models from several sources and perhaps at different times, but he seems to have acquired them well in advance of his death and burial, for there is evidence that many, if not all, had been stored in some accessible place for an appreciable length of time. Dead spiders and cobwebs, and the nests, gnawings, and droppings of mice, which were obvious on at least half of the models, could well have got on them after the sealing of the *sirdāb*. The Theban necropolis must have been infested with mice which made their way through fissures in the rocks and lived on the offerings to the dead.[3] But flies never could have survived in the darkened chamber, and some of the models—notably A, B, and C—were liberally spotted with flyspecks which could only have come while they were kept in some light room above ground.

From four of the boats (P, R, T, V) complete riggings had been so badly broken away that nothing was left except parts of the masts and spars of two of them and a few broken cords still tied in place. This wrenching away of the rigging was not done to get the models into the *sirdāb*, for the largest fully rigged boat (N) was easily put in there. Again, smaller parts of various boats were missing, obviously as the result of accident or petty pilfering. We never found part of the mast of Boat X, the metal masthead, part of a spar, and one jaw of the mast crotch of Q, a jaw of the mast crotch of S, the staff from an officer's hand on T, the arm of a man on Y, and the wooden pins from the steering gear of N and Q. Since it is the boats which have suffered these losses, one is tempted to picture small boys playing with them surreptitiously while they were stored in the house of Meket-Rē'. On the other hand, there seem to have been stray bits of the models separated from their proper places and just dumped into the *sirdāb*. For example, between the blocking of the door and Boat Q we found parts of the masts and spars which we assumed belonged to Boats T, V, and X, and which seem to have been put there just before the *sirdāb* door was sealed. If so, they may be taken as evidence of the careless handling of the models when they were carried up to the tomb. The mast of one boat (V) was burned in two, and a wisp or two of burnt straw were in one of the residence models, which would indicate that a torch was used by the burial party, causing the damage to the mast.

Another curious thing about the handling of the models remains to be noted. After we had brought all of them to the Expedition House and had carefully blown the dust from them with a pair of bellows, we saw that they were literally covered with fingerprints, and fine dust was sticking to the paint where the models had been touched by sweaty hands. They were not the fingerprints of any of us, for we had been very careful never to touch any of the models until we had covered our hands with clean handkerchiefs. Clearly we were looking at the fingerprints of those ancient Thebans who had handled the models about four thousand years before.

We also found things which did not fit any of the models of Meket-Rē' stored in his *sirdāb*. One figure of a man, found near Boat Q, was about 19 centimeters high, had both arms raised as though he were hauling a rope, and had one foot up as if to rest it on the gunwale of a vessel. There is no place for such a figure on any model found by us, and it was not found near enough to the entrance of the *sirdāb* to have fallen in by chance, as may have been the case with another stray figure. This second little man was 24 centimeters high, was painted a chocolate brown color, and had a somewhat different look from any of the figures in

Meket-Rē"s models. One outstretched arm, which seemed to belong to him and would make him the lookout who signals the fowlers to haul the rope and shut the bird net, was found outside the *sirdāb* in the tomb passage. Perhaps these men belonged on another set of models, those deposited in the little *sirdāb* which we believe to have been provided for In-yotef. There was also the broken handle of a model axe, which may have belonged with the fragmentary models which we found in the plundered burial chamber.

In another category were a quantity of model tools found inside the Cattle Stable (D). This model was at the back of the *sirdāb* under Residence Model B, and its entire contents were found exactly as they were left by the burial party. The tools found in it had no possible significance there, for all but one are weavers' implements, and although they were near the Weaving Shop (H), they are much larger in scale.[4] One of them is a carpenter's square, and in scale and in workmanship all are like models of carpenters' tools which we found in the plundered burial crypt.

The items which we have been discussing indicate that the models had been in existence for some time before their deposit in the *sirdāb*— long enough for damage and confusion to have resulted. Whether they were walled up in their little chamber before Meket-Rē"s death is open to question. The probability is that they were borne from his residence to the tomb as part of the funeral procession. From their position in the *sirdāb* when we first opened it, it was obvious that the models of the estate must have been brought in first and placed at the back. Then followed the two big offering bearer girls and the smaller group of tenants bringing offerings. The boats came next and were deposited at the front of the *sirdāb*, but then it was found that there was not room for all of them to be placed on the floor. The Granary (F) was not placed for some time, for a reason which escapes us, and so was nearer the entrance than the other estate models. The largest model, that of the Inspection of Cattle (C), seems to have been put in toward the last, after most of the boats were in, for in pushing it back to the spot where we found it, it had knocked over the Sporting Boat (X) and had damaged Yacht T.

Except for the minor injuries which the models suffered, all were in remarkably fresh condition when they were found by us. It will be noted that no harm whatever had been suffered by models A, D, G, K, and M. Only minor, and in many cases trivial, restorations were required by models E, F, H, J, L, P, and S to W. The most serious injuries had befallen models B, C, N, O, Q, X, and Y. In the detailed notes in the Appendix the condition described is that in which the models stood when work was finished on them in the Expedition House in Ḳurneh in 1920. Thus, all restorations described are those made by me personally in the field before the models were divided between the museums of Cairo and New York, at a time when there was every opportunity to find the original position of each figure or object which had fallen from its place. There were no real questions involved in making these repairs. Where there were cracks they were refilled with a gesso made of plaster and glue, as they originally had been, and this gesso was tinted with water color. No other retouching of paint was made anywhere else. In some cases on the boats broken cords had to be pieced out with new thread, and in a very few cases entirely new cords had to be made, but in practically every instance there was ample evidence to guide the restorations made at the time of the discovery. It may safely be said that rarely has any find been made under more auspicious circumstances.

1. Thebes was in rebellion from about 2143 until 2061 B.C. (See Winlock, *Journal of Near Eastern Studies*, II, no. 4, Oct., 1943, pp. 252, 266, 281.)
2. See below, p. 90.
3. Winlock, *The Tomb of Queen Meryet-Amūn at Thebes*, pp. 28, 52.
4. The weaving implements were all made of coniferous wood and included 50 shuttles, lengths 9 to 12.5 cm., the ends tapered and split with a saw; 50 spindles, lengths 15 to 18.5 cm., each whittled out of a single piece of wood; 52 reels (?), lengths 6.3 to 9 cm. The carpenter's square was 15 cm. x 11.5 cm. Cairo Museum, *Livre d'entrée*, 46734; M.M.A. 20.3.14–90.

APPENDIX

CATALOGUE OF THE MODELS

CATALOGUE OF THE MODELS

A. RESIDENCE

PHOTOGRAPHS · Plate 7 in the tomb; plates 9, 10, 12 in detail

DRAWINGS · Plate 55 in the tomb; plates 56, 57 in detail

CAIRO MUSEUM · *Livre d'entrée* 46721

DIMENSIONS · Length 84 cm.; width 42.5 cm.; height (front) 27.5 cm., (back) 39.5 cm.

CONSTRUCTION · The workmanship is excellent. The model is made entirely of coniferous wood. It has not been thickly covered with gesso as is the case in some of the other models, but the paint is applied directly to the wood. The bottom, a heavy block 11 cm. thick, out of which the pond is carved, has shrunk, making it narrower now than the top of the model. The sides, 4 cm. thick, are mortised and tenoned to the bottom, and the corners have mitered joints, masked on top. The doors and window in the exterior back wall are carefully carved. The architraves of the porch are mortised into the walls, and the roof is a separate plank fitted on them; the rainspouts in the gutter are pierced all the way through. The pond is lined, to make it watertight, with a single sheet of copper fastened around the edges with copper nails. The trees are of wood covered with gesso and painted, and their branches, leaves, and fruit are carved separately and doweled into one another. At the base of each tree is a tenon, 3 cm. long, glued into a hole in the bottom block, and the joint around the base is filled with gesso.

CONDITION · This model showed signs of having been stored a long time after it was made, and in some places it was specked by flies. When placed in the tomb muddy fingerprints were left on it, and bits of burnt straw were dropped in it, possibly from a torch. In it there were cobwebs and dead spiders, and all over it there was dirt left by mice, showing that there was water in the pond at the time it was placed in the tomb.

RESTORATIONS · None

LOCATION · In the far right-hand corner of the chamber, on top of the Butcher Shop (E).

B. RESIDENCE

PHOTOGRAPHS · Plate 7 in the tomb; plates 10–12 in detail

DRAWINGS · Plate 55 in the tomb; plates 56, 57 in detail

METROPOLITAN MUSEUM · Acc. no. 20.3.13

DIMENSIONS · Identical with A

CONSTRUCTION · The workmanship is not so good as A, but the makers were doubtless the same in both cases. The construction is like that of A except that the doors and window on the exterior back wall are not so well carved, the rainspouts in the gutter are not pierced all the way through, the garden is not so carefully made, and there is no gesso around the base of the trees.

CONDITION · A heavy fall of rock from the ceiling had broken most of the trees. There were the same traces of fingerprints, etc., as on A.

RESTORATIONS · The trees were removed to repair them and were then put back in place.

LOCATION · In the middle of the back of the chamber, on top of the Cattle Stable (D).

C. INSPECTION OF CATTLE

PHOTOGRAPHS · Plates 4–6 in the tomb; plates 13–16 in detail

DRAWINGS · Plate 55 in the tomb; plate 58 in detail

CAIRO MUSEUM · *Livre d'entrée* 46724

84

CATALOGUE OF THE MODELS

DIMENSIONS · *Entire model:* length 175 cm.; width 72 cm.; height (back wall) 20–22 cm. *Pavilion:* length 55 cm.; width 19.5 cm.; height 55.5 cm.; width of stairs 7.5 cm.; height of platform 12 cm.; height of parapet 1.5 cm.; height from floor to ceiling 30 cm. *Twenty-six men:* average height 22 cm. *Nineteen cattle:* average height at shoulder 13.2 cm., except large black bull which is 17 cm. high.

CONSTRUCTION · The workmanship is the crudest of all the models. Several of the figures, including Meket-Rēꜥ and his son, are very much like those on the Sporting Boat (X). The wood is for the most part sycamore, and the pegs acacia. The bottom of the model is made of rather rough sycamore boards, 3 cm. thick, held together with three cleats underneath. The numerous cracks are filled with bits of wood and gesso. A crack had appeared after the model was made, and this was roughly plastered and the model was partly repainted after the figures were in position. The bodies of the animals are each carved from one piece of sycamore wood; the legs, sometimes of coniferous wood, are mortised and the horns, ears, and tails pegged in place. The men are made of coniferous wood, with feet carved in one piece with the legs. Both men and animals are covered with gesso and rather carelessly painted, and the men are then varnished.

CONDITION · A large stone had fallen from the ceiling on the rear right-hand corner of the model, splitting it off, and straining and partly separating the boards throughout. The boards had warped, widening some of the cracks, and the gesso in them was often pulverized. Smaller stones from the ceiling had loosened most of the men and animals, and a few of the latter had fallen off behind the model onto the floor of the chamber.

RESTORATIONS · The ground and pavilion had to be largely taken apart because of chips of stone in the cracks. They were then reassembled, with new gesso added where necessary. All figures in place, or near their places, were numbered and their positions noted before removal from the tomb. The placing of the few remaining figures could easily be determined by the peg holes. Minor repairs had to be made on both white animals with small black spots and the right horn of the large red animal. Some of the men's arms needed reattachment.

LOCATION · On top of the models at the back of the chamber, one end resting on the Brewery and Bakery (G), and the other on the Sporting

Boat (X). The Sporting Boat was upset in the process of sliding this large model into the chamber.

D. CATTLE STABLE

PHOTOGRAPHS · Plate 7 in the tomb; plate 17 in detail

DRAWINGS · Plate 55 in the tomb; plate 59 in detail

METROPOLITAN MUSEUM · Acc. no. 20.3.9

DIMENSIONS · *Building:* length 72.5 cm.; width 57 cm.; height 28.5 cm. *Cattle:* average height at shoulder 18 cm., except small brown animal which is 15 cm. high

CONSTRUCTION · The workmanship is crude. The building is made of sycamore boards 2.5 cm. thick, not mitered at the corners, and without cleats on the bottom. The figures and accessories are made of coniferous wood. The paint is applied more carelessly than on any other models except C and H.

CONDITION · Perfect

RESTORATIONS · None

LOCATION · In the back of the chamber on the floor between the Butcher Shop (E) and the Weaving Shop (H), well protected by Residence B, which was placed on top of it. The front half of the stable, which was next to the Weaving Shop, was filled with tools which did not belong in either model (see p. 79).

E. BUTCHER SHOP

PHOTOGRAPHS · Plate 7 in the tomb; plates 18, 19, 21, 24 in detail

DRAWINGS · Plate 55 in the tomb; plates 60, 61 in detail

METROPOLITAN MUSEUM · Acc. no. 20.3.10

DIMENSIONS · *Building:* length 76 cm.; width 58 cm.; height (back) 45.5 cm., (front) 51.5 cm. *Men:* average height 22 cm.

CONSTRUCTION · Made of sycamore boards 2.5 cm. thick. The bottom is held together by two cleats. The roof, which completely covered the building, was added after the model was made and painted, and the cracks between roof and walls were stopped up with gesso and roughly painted with a black hair brush. The figures of the men are made of coniferous wood, the cattle probably being of sycamore. The feet of some of the men are cut out of the same wood as the legs, and the others are modeled in gesso.

CONDITION · Having a roof, it had escaped practically all damage. The outer door had fallen down when the model was put in the chamber, and mice had nested on it and gnawed it. The cords on which the meat was strung, most of which remained, had fallen in pieces and could not support the meat. The duck had fallen out of the hands of the man plucking it.

RESTORATIONS · The roof was removed to repair the interior. The meat strings were copied exactly, and the joints of meat were restrung in the order in which they lay. The duck was put back in the hands of the man plucking it.

LOCATION · In the far right-hand corner of the chamber on the floor under Residence A.

F. GRANARY

PHOTOGRAPHS · Plate 5 in the tomb; plates 20, 21, 24 in detail

DRAWINGS · Plate 55 in the tomb; plates 62, 63 in detail

METROPOLITAN MUSEUM · Acc. no. 20.3.11

DIMENSIONS · *Building:* length 74 cm., width 58 cm., height 36.5 cm. *Men:* average height 20 cm.

CONSTRUCTION · The model is carefully made and painted. The building is constructed of sycamore boards, 2.5–3 cm. thick, with mitered corners and two cleats underneath. The figures and accessories are of coniferous wood. The men's legs end in pegs driven into holes in the floor, and the feet are modeled separately in gesso.

CONDITION · Before being brought to the tomb the model had been handled a good deal. Muddy water had been splashed on it, possibly during the building of the brick wall which sealed up the *sirdāb*. Mouse droppings in the grain in the bins may have come either before or after the model was placed in the tomb. Some damage was caused to the figures by falling stones from the ceiling of the chamber. A man from Boat N had fallen into the corridor of the model.

87

RESTORATIONS · The man carrying a grain sack on his back was mended. A few arms and the five sacks in the hands of the men dumping grain into the bins were put back in place.

LOCATION · On the floor just inside and to the left of the door of the chamber, partially covered by Traveling Boat N.

G. BREWERY AND BAKERY

PHOTOGRAPHS · Plate 7 in the tomb; plates 22–24 in detail

DRAWINGS · Plate 55 in the tomb; plates 64, 65 in detail

METROPOLITAN MUSEUM · Acc. no. 20.3.12

DIMENSIONS · *Building:* length 73 cm., width 55 cm., height 29 cm. *Men and women:* average height 21 cm.

CONSTRUCTION · The building is made of sycamore boards, 2.5 cm. thick, with mitered corners and two cleats underneath. The figures and accessories are of coniferous wood. The feet of the men are modeled in gesso; those of the women are carved out of the same wood as the legs.

CONDITION · Perfect

RESTORATIONS · None

LOCATION · In the far left-hand corner of the chamber on top of the Weaving Shop (H). The Inspection of Cattle (C) was placed above it and protected it from stones falling from the ceiling.

H. WEAVING SHOP

PHOTOGRAPHS · Plate 7 in the tomb; plates 24–27 in detail

DRAWINGS · Plate 55 in the tomb; plates 66, 67 in detail

CAIRO MUSEUM · *Livre d'entrée* 46723

DIMENSIONS · *Building:* length 93 cm., width 45 cm., height 25 cm. *Women:* average height about 17 cm.

CONSTRUCTION · The workmanship is crude. The building is made of sycamore boards, 2.5–3 cm. thick, without mitered corners and without cleats underneath. The figures and accessories are of coniferous wood. The feet of the women are carved in one piece with their legs. There are a number of superfluous peg holes in the floor for which there are neither figures nor objects. The paint on the figures is carelessly applied.

CONDITION · The threads in the hands of the women spinning and stretching the warp were broken in places. One of the round wooden balls representing balls of spun thread had shifted, but its position was shown by the glue on the floor.

RESTORATIONS · The triple threads from the pots to the spinners' hands were glued back in their hands.

LOCATION · In the far left-hand corner of the chamber on the floor under the Brewery and Bakery (G), which effectually protected it.

J. CARPENTER SHOP

PHOTOGRAPHS · Plate 7 in the tomb; plates 21, 24, 28, 29 in detail

DRAWINGS · Plate 55 in the tomb; plates 68, 69 in detail

CAIRO MUSEUM · *Livre d'entrée* 46722
Selection of tools from tool chest in Metropolitan Museum, Acc. nos. 20.3.91–98

DIMENSIONS · *Building:* length 66 cm., width 52 cm., height 26.5 cm. *Men:* average height about 20 cm.

CONSTRUCTION · The building is made of sycamore boards, 2–2.5 cm. thick, with two cleats underneath; the corners are not mitered. The roof was added after the model was made, as in the case of the Butcher Shop (E). A peg hole in the floor in front of the tool chest was probably a mistake of the maker; no object or figure was found for it. The men and the timbers on which they are at work are of coniferous wood. The feet of the men are carved in one piece with their legs. The blades of the tools are copper. The chisel in the hand of the man putting mortise holes in a plank did not fit exactly, and therefore an extra wedge was added; a wedge was also placed behind his foot to keep him seated upright on the plank. The ends of the planks of the big tool chest are mitered, with tongues on the side boards overlapping the ends, but the bottom of the box lacks the cleats which would be necessary to hold the planks together. The lid of the chest is held in place at the back by means of two pegs in the cleat on its underside which slide into holes in that end of the chest, and in front it is fastened by a cord wrapped round and round two knobs, one on the lid and the other on the front end of the chest. This tie is sealed with a dab of clay bearing the impression of a scarab.

CONDITION · Fingerprints were noted around the edge where someone's hands touched it when it was carried to the tomb. There were bits of reed and some mud in the model, perhaps splashed inside by the brick layers who built the sealing of the door. The damage from falling stone was slight.

RESTORATIONS · The right arm and the adze of the man nearest the door of the shop were repaired. The left thumb of the next man was put back in place. The man sawing planks was put upright on his feet, both of which were mended, and the saw handle was put back in his hand. The grinders were glued in place on the beam, where spots of the ancient glue showed they belonged. The mallet in the hand of the man cutting mortises was repaired. The tool chest was opened by withdrawing one peg, and this was put back after the tools had been removed.

LOCATION · On the floor of the chamber in front of the Butcher Shop (E), with the Fishing Canoes (Y) placed on top of it, partially protecting it.

K. OFFERING BEARER BRINGING DRINK

PHOTOGRAPHS · Plates 4–7 in the tomb; plates 30, 31 in detail

DRAWINGS · Plate 55 in the tomb

CAIRO MUSEUM · *Livre d'entrée 46725*

DIMENSIONS · Height (figure) 85.5 cm., (pedestal) 8 cm., (over-all) 122 cm. Pedestal: length 47 cm., width 16.7 cm. Basket: length 20.5 cm., width 18.5 cm., height 16.5 cm.

CONSTRUCTION · The workmanship is excellent. The entire figure is made of coniferous wood. All joints are glued. The head, body, legs, and right foot are in one piece; the front part of the left foot and the arms are added. Tenons under the feet are set into the pedestal and pegged through from the side. The arms are pegged on. The body of the duck is in one piece and the wings in another, the two being joined by a long peg which runs through the girl's hand. The basket is an open box; its sides, mitered at the corners, are 1 cm. thick, and the bottom is 3 cm. thick. In placing it on the girl's head, the maker got his pegs in the wrong place and had to saw them off. Gesso is used on the wig and the offerings only; the rest of the painting is on the bare wood.

CONDITION · Fingerprints were very evident on the statue and its base, and the top of the pedestal had been splashed with muddy water.

RESTORATIONS · None

LOCATION · In the far left-hand corner of the chamber, facing Offering Bearer L, which stood on the opposite side of the room.

L. OFFERING BEARER BRINGING FOOD

PHOTOGRAPHS · Plates 3, 4 in the tomb; plates 30, 31 in detail

DRAWINGS · Plate 55 in the tomb

METROPOLITAN MUSEUM · Acc. no. 20.3.7

DIMENSIONS · Height (figure) 86 cm., (pedestal) 8 cm., (over-all) 112 cm. Pedestal: length 46.5 cm., width 16.7 cm. Basket: length 20 cm., width 19 cm., height 16 cm.

CONSTRUCTION · Same as Offering Bearer K, except that the basket has a false bottom 3 cm. below the rim, and the contents are piled on it. A peg runs through the girl's left hand to balance the basket, and the duck is made as in model K.

CONDITION · A falling stone had broken the basket loose from its pegs but had wedged it in place so that it was still in position, and had also broken the leg of beef and loosened the rib joint. The duck had been knocked out of the girl's hand. Fingerprints were very evident, and the top of the pedestal was spotted with muddy water.

RESTORATIONS · A slight repair was made on the corner of the basket. The hoof was glued on the leg of beef, and the ribs of beef were re-pegged in place. The duck was put back in the girl's hand.

LOCATION · On the right side of the chamber, facing Offering Bearer K on the opposite side of the room.

M. PROCESSION BRINGING OFFERINGS

PHOTOGRAPHS · Plate 7 in the tomb (between the models at center right); plate 32 in detail

DRAWINGS · Plate 55 in the tomb

METROPOLITAN MUSEUM · Acc. no. 20.3.8

DIMENSIONS · *Pedestal:* length 47.5 cm., width 7.2 cm., height 3 cm. *Figures:* height 24 cm.

CONSTRUCTION · The pedestal is made of sycamore, and the figures of coniferous wood. The feet of three of the figures are modeled in gesso; those of the first woman are carved in one piece with the legs. The right hand of the second man was drilled through but never held any object.

CONDITION · There were fingerprints on the pedestal, the *hes* vase, and the head of the first man.

RESTORATIONS · None

LOCATION · On the floor at the back of the chamber, between the Cattle Stable (D) and the Butcher Shop (E).

N. TRAVELING BOAT—SAILING

PHOTOGRAPHS · Plate 4 in the tomb; plates 33, 34, 38, 39, 42 in detail

DRAWINGS · Plate 55 in the tomb; plates 70, 71 in detail

CAIRO MUSEUM · *Livre d'entrée* 46720

DIMENSIONS · *Hull:* length (over-all) 122 cm., (water line) 40 cm., (with rudder) 163 cm.; width (beam) 36 cm.; height (bow) 26 cm., (amidships) 17.5 cm., (stern) 37.5 cm. *Rigging: mast:* height (above deck) 81.3 cm., diameter (at base) 2 cm., (at truck) 1 cm.; *spars:* length 67 cm., greatest diameter 1.5 cm., least diameter 0.7 cm.; *sail:* width 62 cm., height 43.5 cm. *Men:* average height 22–23 cm.

CONSTRUCTION · The hull is carved from a single block of sycamore wood, the cabin is of thin sycamore boards, and the mast stepping and rudder oar are of oak (?); all other accessories and the figures are of coniferous wood. The fittings at the masthead are of copper. The feet of the men are modeled separately in gesso.

CONDITION · The boat had been tipped over by a stone which had fallen on it from the ceiling and had damaged the rigging and the figures, as follows: *Cabin:* Loops of cord for the upper pivots of the cabin doors were broken. *Steering gear:* All ropes had become loosened; the pin in the stern lashing of the rudder was missing; the rudder post and tiller were broken. *Mast and spars:* The mast had fallen out and was crushed in the middle. The two spars were broken. *Rigging:* The forestay was broken off at the bow. The backstay was complete, and the coil on the end reached exactly to the tiller and fitted around it when the latter was put back in place. Stays: loops in rings on the middle hoop on the mast existed; the remainder was lacking. Yard slings: four on starboard side were unbroken; the others had parted. Halyards: ends of four were found tied to each yard arm; other ends were found passing through the hands of five men standing at the foot of the mast and were tied around the mast itself. Yard braces: free ends of cord found on each end of yard; bits of white cord, tied to the horn on the rudder post, could be nothing else but the ends of these braces. *Figures:* Men had fallen on the granary and behind it, and bits of them were thrown and crushed against the door blocking. The arms of many of them had been knocked off. *Hull:* There was one muddy hand print on the hull.

RESTORATIONS · *Cabin:* Loops of cord for upper pivots of cabin doors restored. *Steering gear:* Top lashing of rudder rewrapped; new pin for stern lashing of rudder made; rudder post and tiller mended. *Mast and spars:* Mended. *Rigging:* Forestay: new cord continued from the lower end, where it was broken, to the bow. Backstay: coil on the end slipped over the end of the mended tiller. Stays: two sets of stays restored entirely. As there were no holes through the men's hands, the stays were wrapped around them. Shrouds: entirely restored. Yard slings: all but the four unbroken ones were tied together as far as possible with black thread. Halyards: new string tied over old knots on yard arm and brought down and tied to broken ends of original cords in the hands of the men hauling them. In order to support the weight of the sail and the yard without putting any strain on the remaining parts of the old halyards, the restored halyards were knotted in the ring on the masthead. Yard braces: new cord was tied to the existing part of the port brace and carried back to the fragment on the horn on the rudder post; the starboard brace was entirely restored. *Figures:* All the feet and many of the arms of the men were reglued.

LOCATION · Just inside the entrance, on top of the Granary (F). Doubtless it had been placed upright but was knocked over later by a falling stone from the ceiling. Bow pointed west.

93

MODELS FROM THE TOMB OF MEKET-RĒ'

O. TRAVELING BOAT–ROWING

PHOTOGRAPHS · Plates 5, 7 in the tomb; plates 35, 38, 39, 43 in detail

DRAWINGS · Plate 55 in the tomb; plates 72, 77, 84 in detail

METROPOLITAN MUSEUM · Acc. no. 20.3.1

DIMENSIONS · *Hull:* length (over-all) 128 cm., (water line) 47.5 cm., (with rudder) 175 cm.; width (beam) 29.5 cm.; height (bow) 25 cm., (amidships) 15.5 cm., (stern) 37 cm. *Men:* average height 19 cm.

CONSTRUCTION · Identical with N

CONDITION · The cabin was crushed by two large stones which had fallen from the ceiling, badly splintering and warping it. The entire steering gear was knocked off. The cord on the bumper, the chair, and the gut strings and bridge on the harp were all broken.

RESTORATIONS · The cabin was reassembled, but warping made some insignificant differences in its dimensions. The top lashing on the rudder (original) was rewrapped, and the preventer line was restored. The cord on the bumper was restored. Some unimportant mending was done on the figures of the men.

LOCATION · In the center of the chamber on the floor, partially covered by the Inspection of Cattle (C), and by the Sporting Boat (X) and the Fishing Canoes (Y). Bow pointed west.

P. TRAVELING BOAT–SAILING

PHOTOGRAPHS · Plate 5 in the tomb; plates 36, 38 in detail

DRAWINGS · Plate 55 in the tomb; plate 73 in detail

CAIRO MUSEUM · *Livre d'entrée* 46719

DIMENSIONS · *Hull:* length (over-all) 112 cm., (water line) 37.5 cm., (with rudder) 151.5 cm.; width (beam) 29.5 cm.; height (bow) 24 cm., (amidships) 14.5 cm., (stern) 33 cm. *Men:* average height 20 cm.

CONSTRUCTION · Identical with N

CONDITION · Almost perfect. The boat had been rigged, but the mast, spars, and practically all ropes were missing. One of the preventer lines on the rudder and the cord on the bumper were broken.

94

RESTORATIONS · The preventer line and the bumper cord were mended.

LOCATION · In near left-hand corner of the chamber, partly under Boat R. Bow pointed west.

Q. TRAVELING BOAT–ROWING

PHOTOGRAPHS · Plate 4 in the tomb; plates 37, 38 in detail

DRAWINGS · Plate 55 in the tomb; plate 74 in detail

METROPOLITAN MUSEUM · Acc. no. 20.3.2

DIMENSIONS · *Hull:* length (over-all) 117 cm., (water line) 36 cm., (with rudder) 157 cm.; width (beam) 27 cm.; height (bow) 20.5 cm., (amidships) 13.7 cm., (stern) 30.5 cm. *Rigging: mast:* height 78 cm.; diameter (at base) 2.2 cm., (at truck) 0.9 cm.; *spars:* length 66 cm., greatest diameter 1 cm., least diameter 0.6 cm.; *sail:* 65 x 42 cm. *Men:* average height of sailors 18 cm., of officers 20.5 cm.

CONSTRUCTION · Identical with N

CONDITION · A heavy piece of stone from the ceiling had fallen on the stern, upending the boat and damaging it as follows: *Cabin:* Roof broken. *Steering gear:* The top lashing of the rudder was broken, the pin in the stern lashing was missing, and the preventer line was snarled around the rudder. *Mast and spars:* The mast was broken and lay near the door of the chamber; the metal head was missing. The crotch was broken, and one jaw was missing. The spars, one of which was broken and part of it missing, also lay near the door. There is no definite proof that the mast and spars belong to this boat except that they almost surely go together and that they are the right size for the sail, which was found folded up on the deck. They may have been thrown off the boat when it was upended. *Oars:* The oars had been knocked out and lay under stone chip, and all but three of the oarlock cords were broken. *Figures:* Many of them had been knocked off the boat when it was upended and lay under chips of stone, with most of their arms and legs broken.

RESTORATIONS · *Cabin:* Roof mended. *Steering gear:* The top lashing of the rudder was mended and put back, the pin in the stern lashing was restored, and the preventer line was put back in place. *Mast and spars:* The mast and spars were mended and were laid in the crotch, as they probably originally were, for one photograph. *Oars:* The oars were put lengthwise through the oarlock loops for one photograph and in the men's hands for the other. The oarlock cords were restored. *Figures:* The arms and legs of most of the men were mended.

LOCATION · In the center of the chamber between Boat O and the Granary (F). Bow pointed east.

R. KITCHEN TENDER—SAILING

PHOTOGRAPHS · Plate 5 in the tomb; plates 40, 42, 44 in detail

DRAWINGS · Plate 55 in the tomb; plates 75, 77, 84 in detail

CAIRO MUSEUM · *Livre d'entrée* 46718

DIMENSIONS · *Hull:* length (over-all) 117 cm., (water line) 36 cm., (with rudder) 156 cm.; width (beam) 30.8 cm.; height (bow) 28 cm., (amidships) 15 cm., (stern) 35 cm. *Men:* average height 22 cm.

CONSTRUCTION · Practically identical with N, so far as the ship itself goes.

CONDITION · This boat must originally have been fully rigged. The mast stepping still had lashings around it where the foot of the mast had been; in holes provided for them in either side of the gunwale opposite the mast there were bits of the shrouds; and fragments of ropes were held in the hands of the men hauling the halyards. However, the mast and rigging had been torn out, breaking all the ropes. The mast, spars, and sail were missing, and of the rigging only a snarl of black and white ropes remained on the deck. The preventer line of the rudder was broken where it crossed the gunwale, and the bumper cord was broken. The cabin had fallen off the boat, the strings for the meat had broken, and the meat was lying on the deck. Apparently by an oversight there was nothing to which to attach the strings of meat in the back of the cabin, and it would seem that the meat had always been lying there.

RESTORATIONS · The preventer line was pieced out with a small bit of cord, and the bumper cord was restored. The strings for the meat were restored, and because there was nothing to attach them to in the back of the cabin, these cords were fastened to the rudder post for the detailed photographs shown on Plate 44, before the cabin was put back in place.

LOCATION · Just inside the chamber to the left, partly on top of Traveling Boat P, and partly supported under the stern by two bricks like those used for sealing the entrance to the chamber. Bow pointed west.

CATALOGUE OF THE MODELS

S. KITCHEN TENDER—ROWING

PHOTOGRAPHS · Plate 7 in the tomb; plates 41, 43, 44 in detail

DRAWINGS · Plate 55 in the tomb; plates 76, 77, 86 in detail

METROPOLITAN MUSEUM · Acc. no. 20.3.3

DIMENSIONS · *Hull:* length (over-all) 127 cm., (water line) 50 cm., (with rudder) 147 cm.; width (beam) 33 cm.; height (bow) 28 cm., (amidships) 16.5 cm., (stern) 40 cm. *Men and women:* average height 20 cm.

CONSTRUCTION · Identical with Kitchen Tender R. The feet of the women are carved in one piece with the legs and are attached to the deck with pegs.

CONDITION · When the Inspection of Cattle (C) was broken the steering gear of this boat was knocked off, breaking all the ropes except the lashing at the top of the rudder. One jaw of the mast crotch was missing, and the oarlock cords and the bumper cord were broken. The poker from the hand of the man tending the fire in the oven was missing.

RESTORATIONS · The stern lashing and the preventer line on the rudder were restored on the basis of the existing fragments. The oars were placed in the hands of the rowers for photographing. The mast crotch, and the oarlock cords and bumper cord were restored.

LOCATION · In the back of the chamber on the floor under the Inspection of Cattle (C), which protected it except in the stern. Bow pointed west.

T. YACHT—SAILING

PHOTOGRAPHS · Plates 4–7 in the tomb; plates 45, 49, 50 in detail. See also plate 1

DRAWINGS · Plate 55 in the tomb; plates 78, 85 in detail

METROPOLITAN MUSEUM · Acc. no. 20.3.4

DIMENSIONS · *Hull:* length (over-all) 145 cm., (water line) 38 cm., (with rudders) 159 cm.; width (beam) 28.5 cm.; height (bow) 45.5 cm., (amidships) 16 cm., (stern) 40 cm. *Rigging: mast:* height (deck to truck) 94 cm., diameter (at base) 2 cm.; *spars:* lengths 78, 80 cm. (both were originally 80 cm., but the shorter had one end broken off anciently). *Men:* average height 23 cm.; steersmen, 20 cm.

CONSTRUCTION · The hull is carved out of a block of sycamore wood, with the bow and stern ornaments carved separately and pegged on. The steering gear, mast and spars, canopy, figures, and accessories are of coniferous wood, except the mooring pegs and mallet, which are of tamarisk. The figures of Meket-Rē' and his son were specially carved of very straight-grained coniferous wood by a master sculptor (see Plate 1).

CONDITION · The stone which had fallen on the Inspection of Cattle (C) had badly damaged the stern, and the Sporting Boat (X) had rolled over on it, breaking the roof of the canopy. *Hull:* The stern post was broken off. *Steering gear:* The port rudder was broken, and the rudder rest was broken off. The lashings of both rudders to the posts and to the rudder rest were broken when the latter was broken off. *Mast and spars:* The mast was found near the door, burned in two about 15 cm. below the head. The metal truck was missing. This mast was certainly in the stepping at one time, for it is whittled away on one side to fit the stepping, and marks of the stepping still show on its foot. The spars, one with an old break at one end, were also found near the door. *Rigging:* The boat had been fully rigged at one time, but the mast had been torn loose, breaking all the ropes, before the boat was put in the tomb. The forestay was tied to the bow post but was lying on the deck, with the loop at its other end, for fastening it to the mast truck, broken. A fragment of the white rope backstay was tied to a black rope ring in the rudder rest, and fragments of black rope backstays were tied to the port rudder post. Ends of sidestays were still tied to loops of rope in the gunwale opposite the canopy, and ends of shrouds were looped through holes in the gunwale opposite the mast. The end of one halyard was found around the upper spar, and fragments of halyards passed through the hands of the men hauling them and then through a loop of cord in the deck. *Figures:* The arms of some of the men were broken, and the scepter in the hand of one of the officers was missing.

RESTORATIONS · *Hull:* The stern post was put back in place. *Steering gear:* Port rudder was mended, rudder rest was reglued, and lashings of rudders to posts were entirely restored. *Mast and spars:* The mast was mended. It was assigned to this boat because its height exactly corresponded to the length of the forestay, its foot fitted the mast stepping, and its decoration was like that on the columns of the canopy. The spars were tied to the mast. *Rigging:* The forestay was tied to the top of the mast, the fragment of backstay in the rudder rest was pieced out to fasten it to the top of the mast, and the halyards in the hands of the men hauling them were pieced out and attached to the masthead. *Cabin:* The roof was mended. *Figures:* The man poling the boat was put back in place on the port side of the deck. The arms of some of the men were mended.

LOCATION · On the floor of the chamber, in the center between Boats O and S. Except for the stern it was protected by the large model of the Inspection of Cattle (C) placed above it. Bow pointed west. The mast and spars were found near the entrance to the chamber.

U. YACHT—PADDLING

PHOTOGRAPHS · Plate 5 in the tomb; plates 46, 49, 50 in detail

DRAWINGS · Plate 55 in the tomb; plates 79, 85, 86 in detail

CAIRO MUSEUM · *Livre d'entrée* 46716

DIMENSIONS · *Hull:* length (over-all) 139 cm., (water line) 40 cm., (with rudders) 140.5 cm.; width (beam) 25 cm.; height (bow) 47 cm., (amidships) 14.5 cm., (stern) 37 cm. *Men:* average height 23–24 cm.; steersmen, 14, 16.5 cm.

CONSTRUCTION · Identical with Yacht T

CONDITION · Almost perfect. The top lashing of the starboard rudder was broken, and the canopy roof and two columns had fallen over. The paddles were found stacked on deck.

RESTORATIONS · The top lashing of the starboard rudder was completely restored. The canopy was put back in place. The mast crotch was put in the stepping, and the paddles were put in the paddlers' hands as they had originally been assembled.

LOCATION · On the floor of the chamber at the left of the entrance between Boats P and W. Bow pointed west.

V. YACHT—SAILING

PHOTOGRAPHS · Plate 5 in the tomb; plate 47 in detail

DRAWINGS · Plate 55 in the tomb; plates 80, 85, 86 in detail

CAIRO MUSEUM · *Livre d'entrée* 46717

DIMENSIONS · *Hull:* length (over-all) 132 cm., (water line) 38 cm., (with rudders) 134.5 cm.; width (beam) 29 cm.; height (bow) 47 cm., (amidships) 16.5 cm., (stern) 33 cm. *Rigging: mast:* two fragments each 22 cm. long. *Men:* average height 22 cm.; steersmen, 17 cm.

CONSTRUCTION · Identical with Yacht T

CONDITION · The boat had originally been fully rigged, but the rigging was missing except for broken cordage and two fragments of the mast, found near the door. A piece was broken off the knob on the stern post. The starboard rudder post and the rudder rest had become unglued. The top lashing of the port rudder was loosened, but the ropes were intact.

RESTORATIONS · The broken piece was put back on the knob of the stern post. The rudder rest and the starboard rudder post were glued in place. The top lashing of the port rudder was rewrapped.

LOCATION · On the floor of the chamber at the left of the entrance between Yachts T and W. Bow pointed west. Pieces of the mast probably belonging to this boat were found near the door.

W. YACHT–PADDLING

PHOTOGRAPHS · Plate 5 in the tomb; plate 48 in detail

DRAWINGS · Plate 55 in the tomb; plates 77, 81, 86 in detail

METROPOLITAN MUSEUM · Acc. no. 20.3.5

DIMENSIONS · *Hull:* length (over-all) 132.5 cm., (water line) 38 cm., (with rudders) 140.5 cm.; width (beam) 30.5 cm.; height (bow) 47.5 cm., (amidships) 17 cm., (stern) 31.5 cm. *Men:* average height 23 cm.; steersmen, 17.5 cm.

CONSTRUCTION · Identical with Yacht T

CONDITION · Almost perfect. The preventer line on the port rudder was broken. The paddles were found stacked on deck, but paint marks show that they were originally held in the hands of the paddlers.

RESTORATIONS · The preventer line on the port rudder was mended. The mast crotch was put in the stepping, and the paddles were placed in the men's hands, as they had originally been assembled.

CATALOGUE OF THE MODELS

LOCATION · On the floor of the chamber at the left of the entrance between Yachts U and V. Bow pointed east.

X. SPORTING BOAT

PHOTOGRAPHS · Plates 5, 6 in the tomb; plates 51, 53 in detail; frontispiece in color

DRAWINGS · Plate 55 in the tomb; plates 82, 83, 86 in detail

METROPOLITAN MUSEUM · Acc. no. 20.3.6

DIMENSIONS · *Hull:* length (over-all) 114.5 cm., (water line) 43 cm., (with rudder) 123.5 cm.; width (beam) 23.5 cm.; height (bow) 19 cm., (amidships) 12 cm., (stern) 26.8 cm. *Men:* average height 22.5–23 cm.; boy with ducks, 20 cm.

CONSTRUCTION · The hull is carved from a block of sycamore. The steering gear, canopy, figures, and accessories are of coniferous wood. The feet of the figures are carved in one piece with the legs. The figures of Meket-Rē᷄ and his son are identical with those in the Inspection of Cattle (C). Some alterations had been made in the placing of the figures, and the old peg holes remained; for example, the man kneeling to land a fish was originally where the girl is. The position of the tiller had been changed, and the mast stepping was twisted out of place to admit the figure on the port side and then cut away on the starboard side. The paddles are a miscellaneous lot of various shapes and conditions.

CONDITION · When the boat was knocked over on its left side at the time the Inspection of Cattle (C) was placed in the chamber, the top of the cabin was broken off but its grilled sides remained in place. The net poles lashed to the port side of the cabin fell off; those on the starboard side remained in place. The net pegs were found lying opposite the stern. The steering oar cleat was unglued. Most of the figures had fallen off the boat, and the arms of many were broken. The strings tying the coots in the boy's hands were broken. The body of the duck in the girl's hand was broken off from the wings. The harpoon reels had fallen off the harpooners' arms.

RESTORATIONS · The top of the cabin was put on. The net poles were tied to the port side of the cabin. The steering oar cleat was reglued. The figures were put back in place, their positions being determined by the peg holes in their feet and in the deck, and by the color of the paint stuck in the glue where their feet had been. Their arms were mended. The punting pole was put back in the bowman's hand. The strings tying the coots in the boy's hands were restored, imitating the old ones exactly. The body of the duck in the girl's hand was put back in place. The oxyrhynchus fish was put on the shoulder of the fisherman standing next to Meket-Rēˁ; something had been glued there and tied with thread to his hand, and this fish seemed to fit. The harpoon reels were hung on the harpooners' arms where glue spots indicated they belonged.

LOCATION · The boat had probably been placed on top of Boats S and T, but it had been rolled over on its side on to Boats O and T by the placing of the Inspection of Cattle (C). Bow pointed northwest. Part of the mast and the mast crotch were found near the entrance.

Y. FISHING CANOES

PHOTOGRAPHS · Plates 3–5 in the tomb; plates 52, 53 in detail

DRAWINGS · Plate 55 in the tomb

CAIRO MUSEUM · *Livre d'entrée* 46715

DIMENSIONS · *Canoes:* lengths 90 and 95 cm.; widths (beam) 15.5 and 18 cm.; heights (bow) 24 and 26 cm., (amidships) 10 and 12 cm., (stern) 23.5 and 32 cm. *Board* (water): length 56 cm., width 30 cm., thickness 2.5 cm. *Men:* average height 20 cm., if standing upright

CONSTRUCTION · Hulls and board (water) are made of sycamore. Both canoes are pegged to the board very carelessly, and the joints around the bottoms are filled with sticks and gesso. The men are made of coniferous wood, their feet carved in one piece with their legs. The outer edge of the trawl, representing the rope around its mouth, is made of wood and the net proper of string, the whole coated with gesso. A peg under the bottom of the net in the board holds the net up at the back. The fish are made of coniferous wood. Marks on the net and on the fish show that the latter were glued inside the bottom of the net.

CONDITION · The model was badly damaged by stones which fell from the ceiling, breaking off all but four of the men and also most of their arms, and partly crushing the net. However, the bottom of the net was intact, and the hands on some loose arms of the men still held the net hauling ropes. The stern post of the smaller canoe was broken off. One man on the larger canoe lacked an arm, which could not be found in the tomb.

RESTORATIONS · The men were put back on the decks according to peg holes and marks there. The arms of most of the men were reattached, but no attempt was made to restore the hauling ropes in their hands. The mouth of the net was put together, a sufficient number of pieces fitting together to give the outline. Since some minute fragments could not be replaced and the net thus held solidly together, it was necessary to mend the body of the net with string and gesso. The position of the net was given by the peg in the board. The stern post of the smaller canoe was put back in place.

LOCATION · At the back of the chamber on the right, on top of the Carpenter Shop (J). Bows pointed east.

REFERENCES CITED

Breasted, James Henry. "The Earliest Boats on the Nile." *The Journal of Egyptian Archaeology*, vol. IV (1917), pp. 174 ff.

Breasted, James Henry, Jr. *Egyptian Servant Statues*. The Bollingen Series XIII. New York, 1948

Clark, Charlotte R. "Egyptian Weaving in 2000 B.C." *The Metropolitan Museum of Art Bulletin*, vol. III, no. 1, Summer, 1944, pp. 24 ff.

Crowfoot, G. M., and H. Ling Roth. "Models of Egyptian Looms." *Ancient Egypt*, 1921, part IV, pp. 97 ff.

Daressy, G. "Trois points inexplorés de la nécropole thébaine." *Annales du Service des Antiquités de l'Égypte*, Tome II, Cairo, 1901, pp. 133 ff.

Erman, Adolph, and Aylward M. Blackman. *The Literature of the Ancient Egyptians*. London, 1927

Faulkner, R. O. "Egyptian Seagoing Ships." *The Journal of Egyptian Archaeology*, vol. 26 (1940), pp. 3 ff.

Gardiner, Alan H. *Egyptian Grammar*. Oxford, 1927

Johl, C. H. *Altägyptische Webestühle und Brettchenweberei in Altägypten* (*Untersuchungen zur Geschichte und Altertumskunde Aegyptens*, VIII. Band). Leipzig, 1924

Morgan, J. de. *Fouilles à Dahchour, mars-juin, 1894*. Vienna, 1895

Naville, Edouard. *The XIth Dynasty Temple at Deir el-Bahari*, part II. London, 1910

Newberry, Percy E. *Beni Hasan* (*Egypt Exploration Fund. Archaeological Survey of Egypt*), part I. London, 1893

Reisner, G. A. *Models of Ships and Boats* (*Catalogue général des antiquités égyptiennes du Musée du Caire*). Cairo, 1913

Roth, H. Ling, and G. M. Crowfoot. "Models of Egyptian Looms." *Ancient Egypt*, 1921, part IV, pp. 97 ff.

Smith, William Stevenson. *Ancient Egypt as Represented in the Museum of Fine Arts*. Boston, 1942

Winlock, H. E. "Digger's Luck." *Scribner's Magazine*, February, 1921, pp. 207 ff.

—— "The Eleventh Egyptian Dynasty." *Journal of Near Eastern Studies*, vol. II, no. 4, October, 1943, pp. 249 ff.

—— *Excavations at Deir el Baḥri, 1911–1931*. New York, 1942

—— "Excavations at Thebes." *Bulletin of The Metropolitan Museum of Art*, vol. XV (1920), December, part II, pp. 12 ff.

—— "Heddle-jacks of Middle Kingdom Looms." *Ancient Egypt*, 1922, part III, pp. 71 ff.

—— "The Museum's Excavations at Thebes." *Bulletin of The Metropolitan Museum of Art*, vol. XIX (1924), December, part II, pp. 5 ff.

—— *The Rise and Fall of the Middle Kingdom in Thebes*. New York, 1947

—— *The Slain Soldiers of Neb-ḥepet-Rēᶜ Mentu-ḥotpe* (*Publications of The Metropolitan Museum of Art Egyptian Expedition*, vol. XVI). New York, 1945

—— *The Tomb of Queen Meryet-Amūn at Thebes* (*Publications of The Metropolitan Museum of Art Egyptian Expedition*, vol. VI). New York, 1932

PLATES

1. Meket-Rē' and his son as represented on Yacht T, in the Metropolitan Museum of Art

2. The entrance to the *sirdāb* of the tomb of Meket-Rē' as we first saw it and after we had uncovered the brick wall which blocked it

3. The brick wall blocking the entrance to the *sirdāb*. Below, the interior of the *sirdāb* as we first saw it, looking over the lower courses of the wall

4. General view of the *sirdāb* with the models in place as we found them

5. Views of the *sirdāb* after the removal of the first of the models

6. The largest model, the Inspection of Cattle (C), in position as it was found

7. Views of the back of the *sirdāb* after the removal of various models

8. Arab workmen carrying the models from the tomb to the Expedition House

9.   Residence A in the Cairo Museum

10. The exteriors of the two models of the residence of Meket-Rē'

11. The porch of Residence B, in New York, and its roof, with the trees in the garden removed

12. The residence models in Cairo (A, left) and New York (B, right) as seen from above, and a tree from the latter

13. The large model (C), the Inspection of Cattle

14. The procession of animals being inspected by Meket-Rēʿ (C)

15. Meket-Rē' and his son, the scribes, and the courtiers as they inspect the cattle from the pavilion, with the head cattleman. (View of model C taken during repair)

16. The scribes, courtiers and head cattleman, and bullocks with their drivers, from the Inspection of Cattle (C)

17. The Cattle Stable (D)

18. The Butcher Shop (E) after its roof had been removed

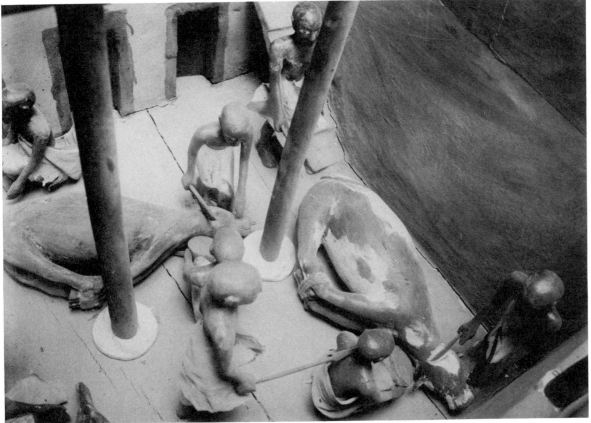

19. Detailed views looking into the courtyard of the Butcher Shop (E)

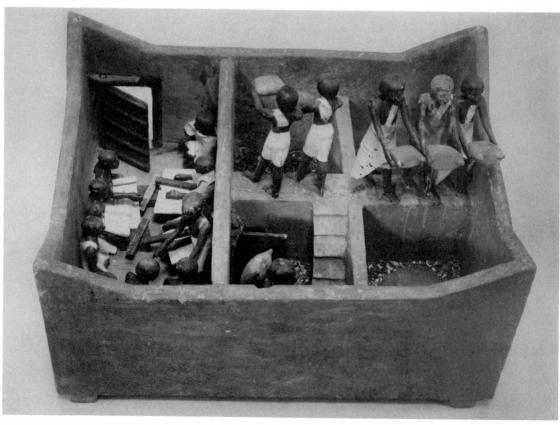

20. The Granary (F)

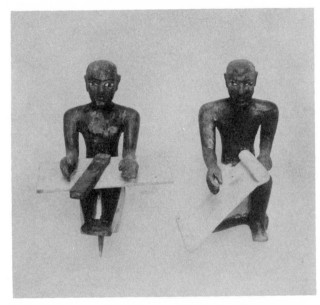

21. Figures from various shop models

22. The Brewery and Bakery (G)

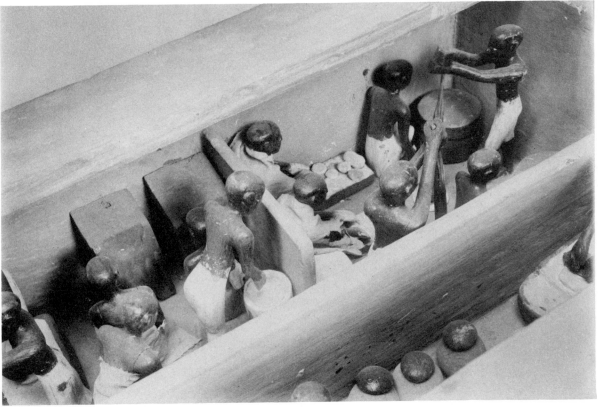

23. Detailed views looking into the Brewery and Bakery (G)

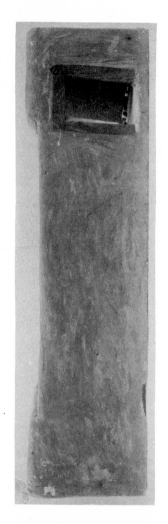

ABOVE:
24. The exteriors of models of buildings

25. The Weaving Shop (H)

26. The interior of the Weaving Shop (H)

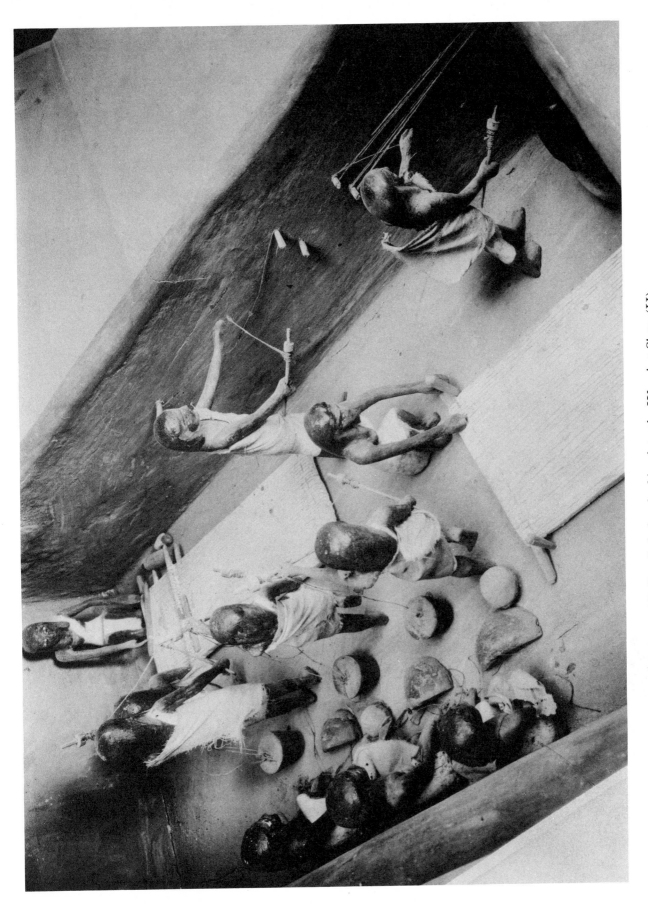

27. Detailed view looking into the Weaving Shop (H)

28. The Carpenter Shop (J)

29. Views of the Carpenter Shop (J)

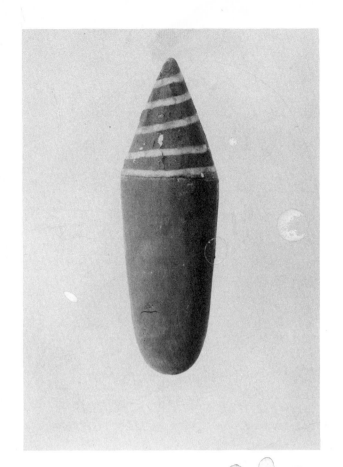 

31. One of the beer jars and the basket of food carried by Offering Bearers K and L

LEFT:

30. Two girls carrying baskets of food and drink to the tomb (K, L)

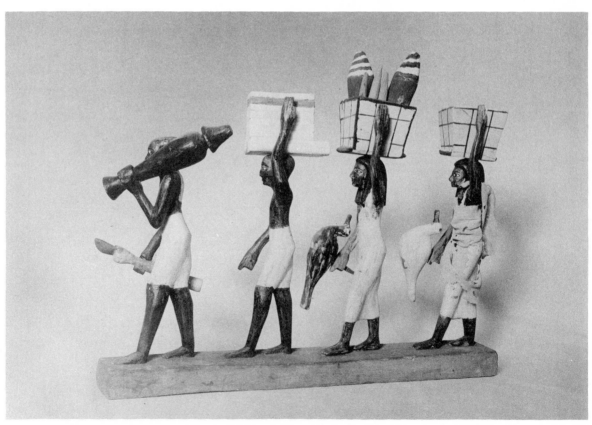

32. The procession of men and women carrying offerings to the tomb (M)

33. Traveling Boat N under sail

34. The crew raising and trimming the sail on Traveling Boat N

35. Traveling Boat O with the oars laid up in the rowlocks, as it was put in the tomb

36. Traveling Boat P with the crew raising and trimming a sail now lost

37. Traveling Boat Q as it was put in the tomb, and as originally assembled

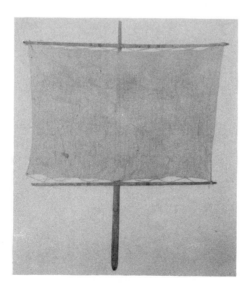

38. Figures and equipment from the traveling boats

39. The cabins from Boats N and O. Below, Meket-Rē' and his musicians from Boat O

40. Kitchen Tender R with the crew raising and trimming a sail now lost

41. Kitchen Tender S being rowed

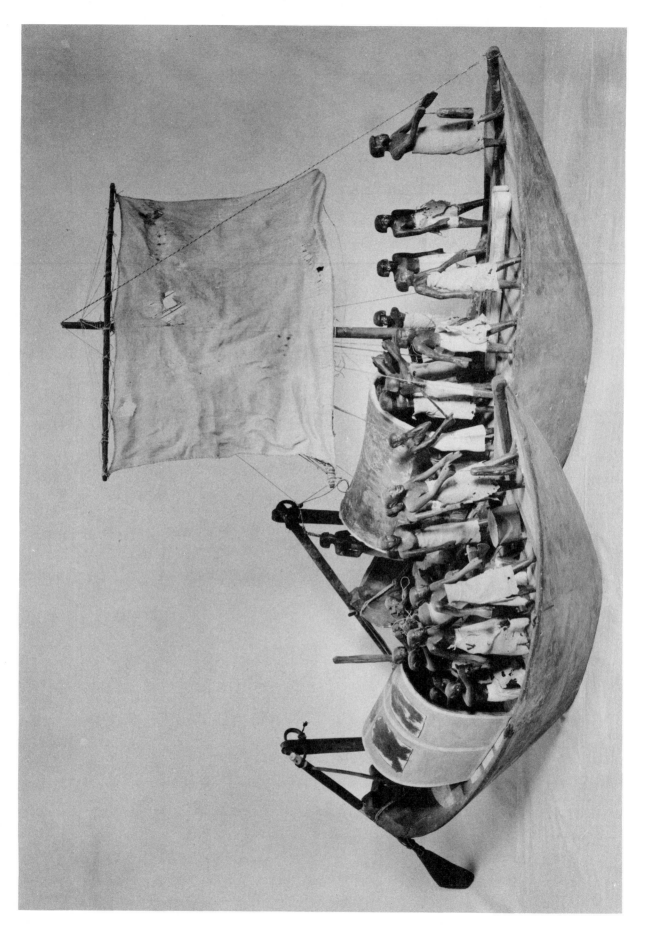

42. Traveling Boat N and Kitchen Tender R in the Cairo Museum

43. Traveling Boat O and Kitchen Tender S in the Metropolitan Museum

44. The cabins removed from Kitchen Tenders R and S to show food supplies stored on deck and cooks at work

45. Yacht T rerigged for sailing as originally assembled, and as it was put in the tomb

46. Yacht U with the paddles stowed on deck as it was put in the tomb, and
with the crew paddling as originally assembled

47. Yacht V with the crew raising and trimming a sail now lost

48. Yacht W with the paddles stowed on deck as it was put in the tomb, and
with the crew paddling as originally assembled

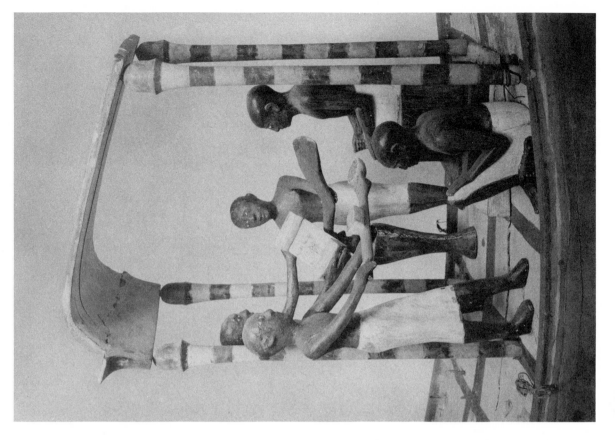

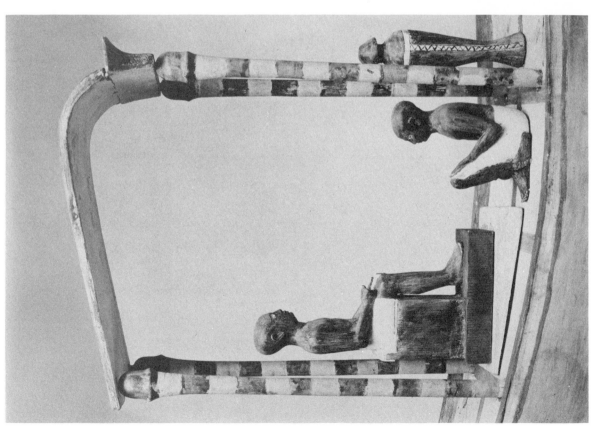

49. Meket-Rēʿ and his son In-yotef seated under the canopies on Yachts U and T

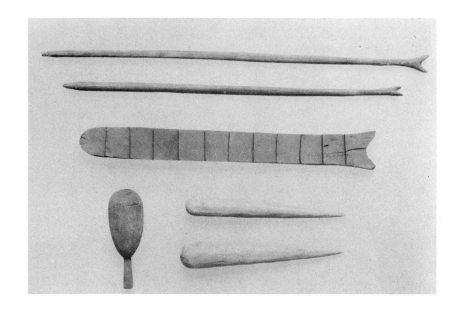

50. Figures and equipment from Yachts T and U

51. The Sporting Boat (X)

52. Two Fishing Canoes (Y) dragging a trawl between them

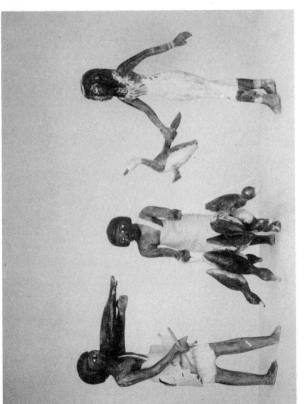

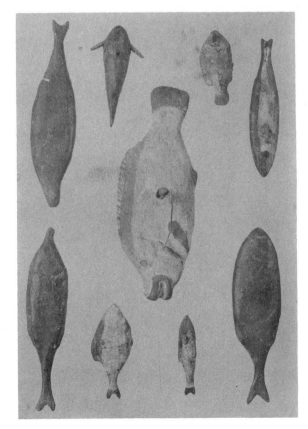

53. Figures and equipment from the Sporting Boat (X) and the Fishing Canoes (Y)

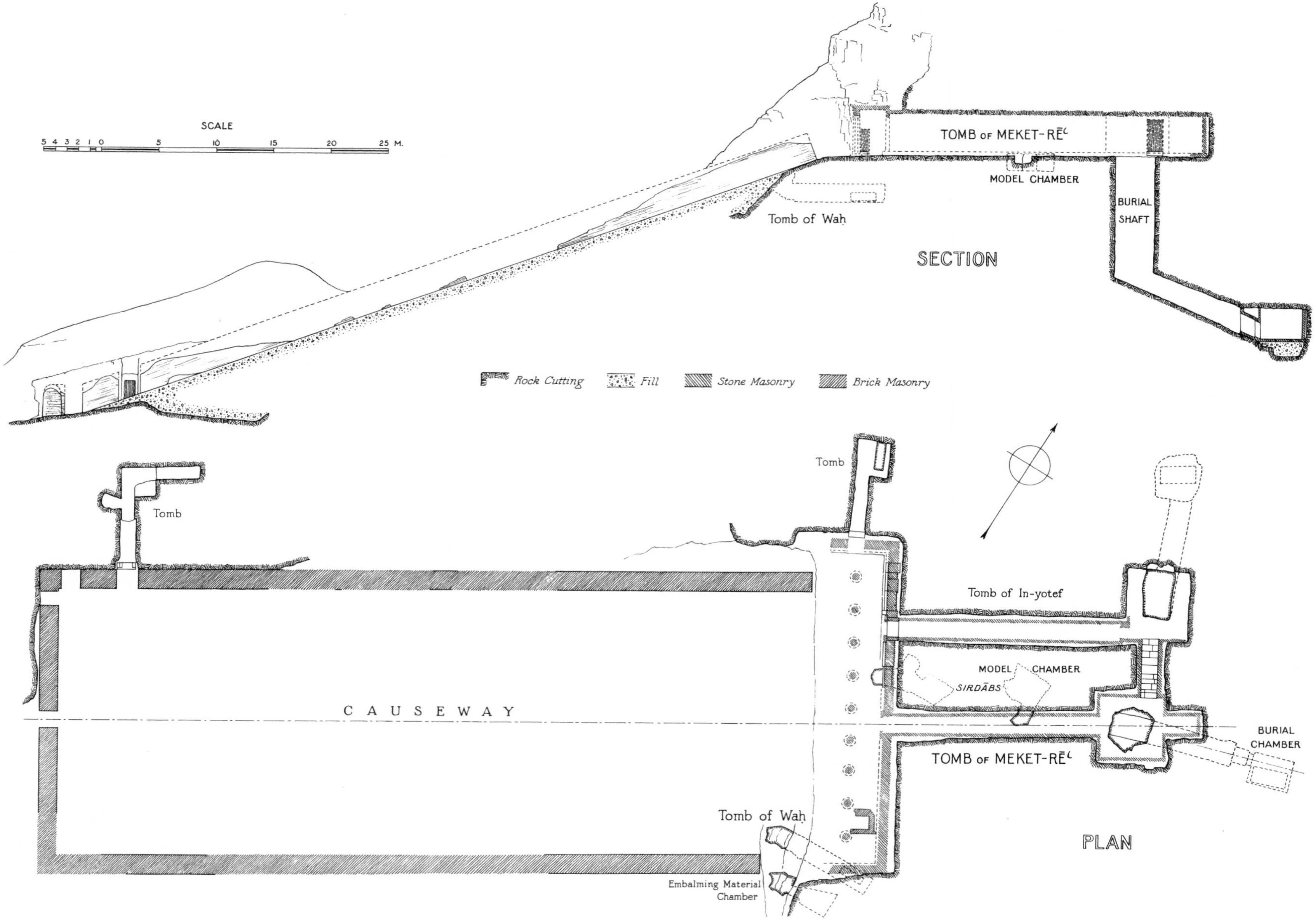

SECTION

TOMB of MEKET-RĒᶜ

MODEL CHAMBER

BURIAL SHAFT

Tomb of Wah

Rock Cutting   Fill   Stone Masonry   Brick Masonry

SCALE

5 4 3 2 1 0   5   10   15   20   25 M.

PLAN

BURIAL CHAMBER

Tomb of In-yotef

MODEL CHAMBER

SIRDĀBS

Tomb

TOMB of MEKET-RĒᶜ

Tomb of Wah

Embalming Material Chamber

Tomb

C A U S E W A Y

54. Plan and section of the tomb of Meket-Rēᶜ

PLAN

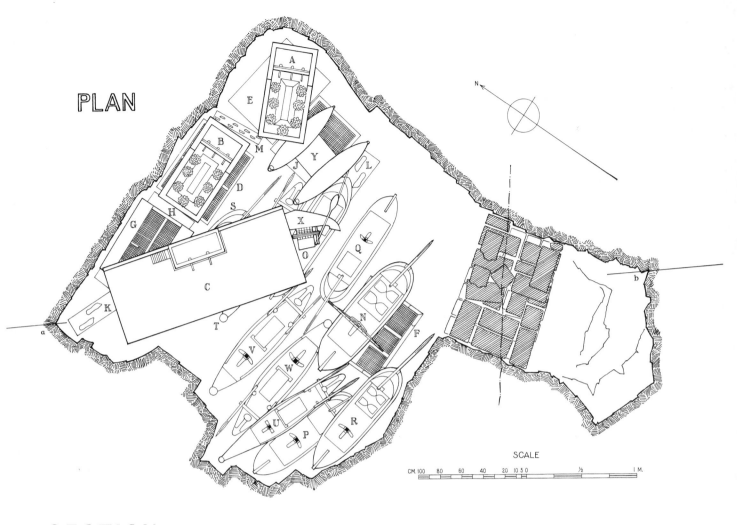

N

SCALE

CM. 100   80   60   40   20 10 5 0   ½   1 M.

SECTION

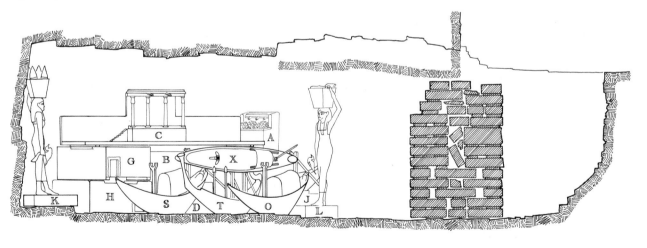

SCALE

1   0   1   2 Meters

55. Plan and section of the *sirdāb* of the tomb of Meket-Rē'

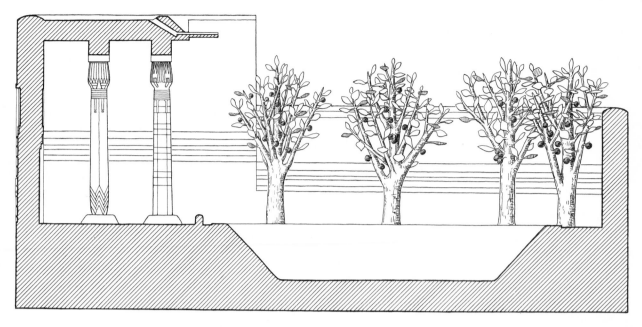

SECTION

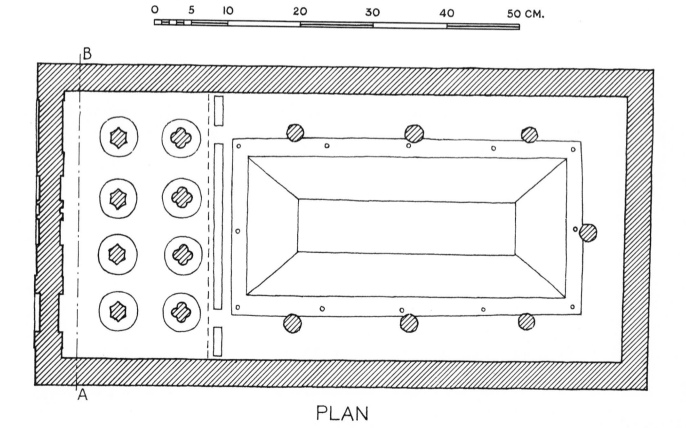

PLAN

56. Models of the Residence (A, B)

END ELEVATION

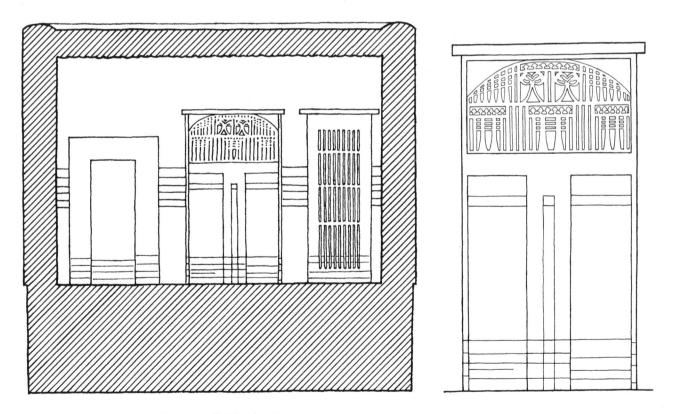

SECTION A-B

57. Details of the models of the Residence (A, B)

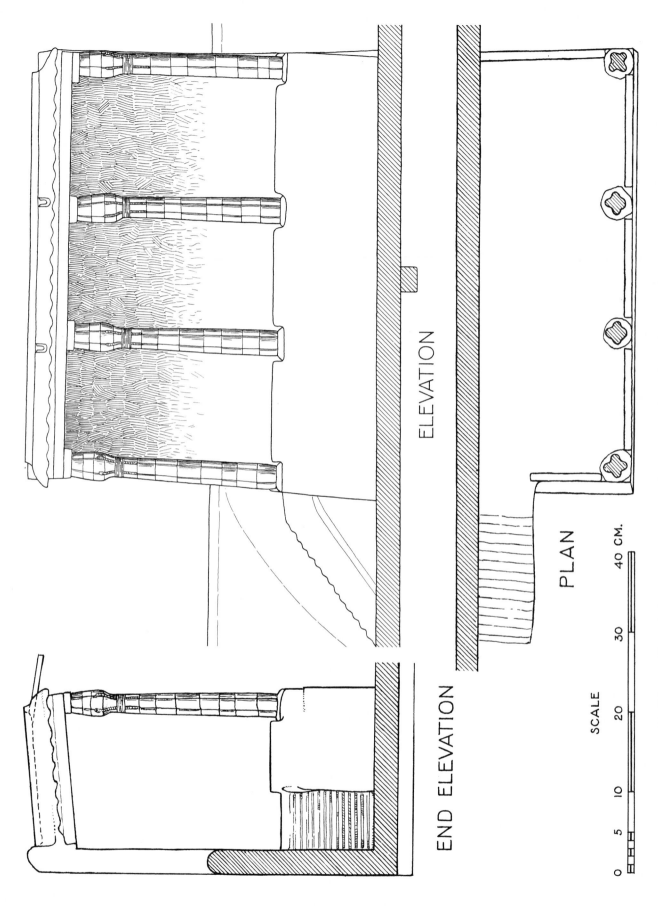

ELEVATION

END ELEVATION

PLAN

SCALE

0   5   10   20   30   40 CM.

58. The pavilion of the model showing Meket-Rēʿ superintending the counting of his cattle (C)

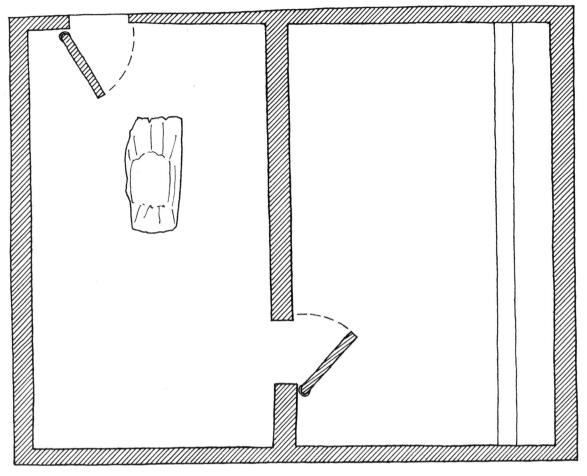

PLAN

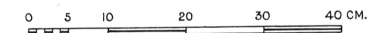

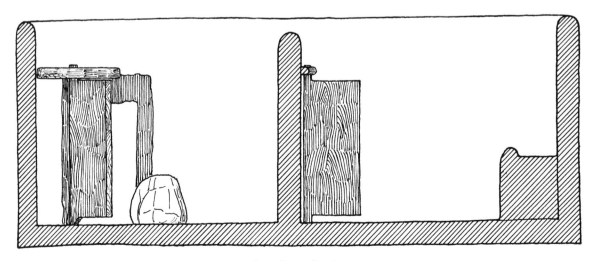

SECTION

59. The Cattle Stable (D)

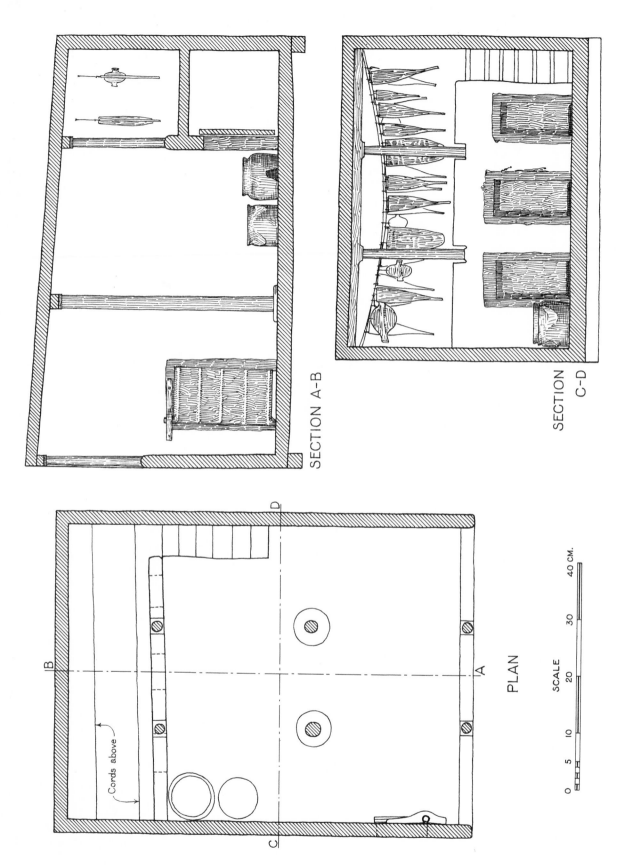

SECTION A-B

SECTION
C-D

PLAN

Cords above

SCALE

0   5   10   20   30   40 CM.

60. The Butcher Shop (E)

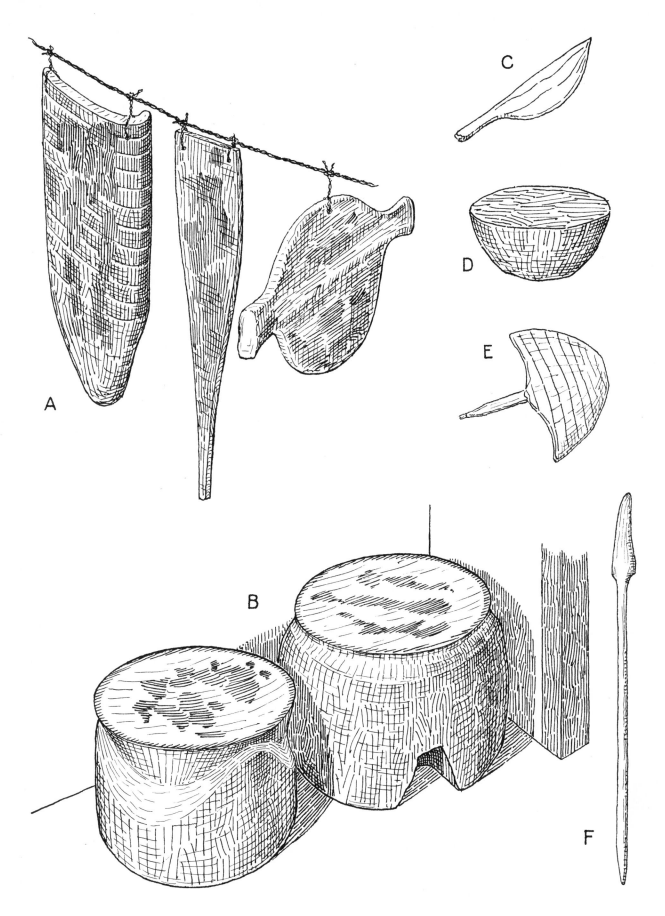

61. Equipment of the Butcher Shop (E)

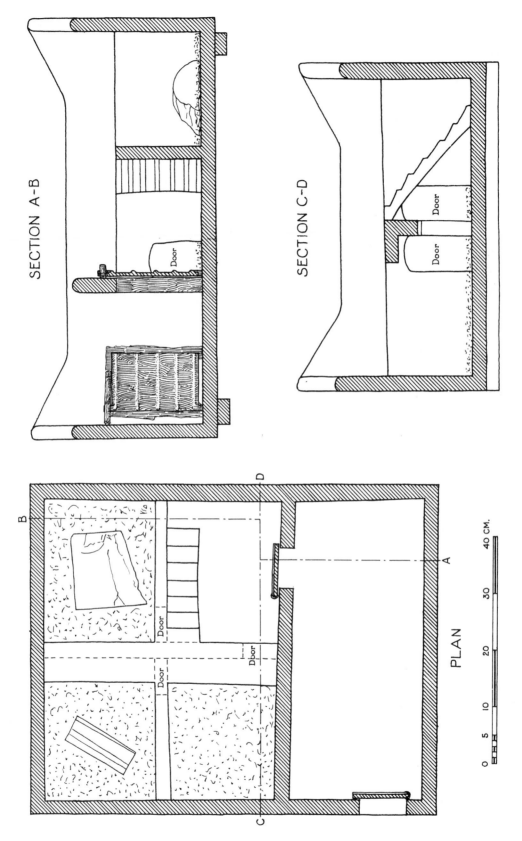

SECTION A-B

SECTION C-D

Door

Door

Door

Door

B

D

C

A

PLAN

0 5 10 20 30 40 CM.

62. The Granary (F)

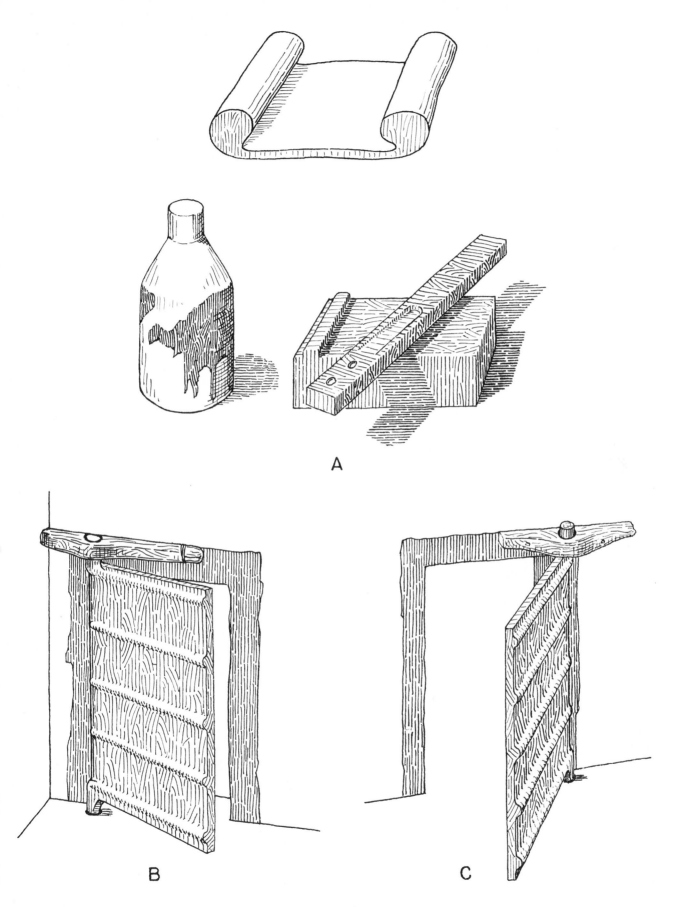

A

B   C

63. Details of the Granary (F)

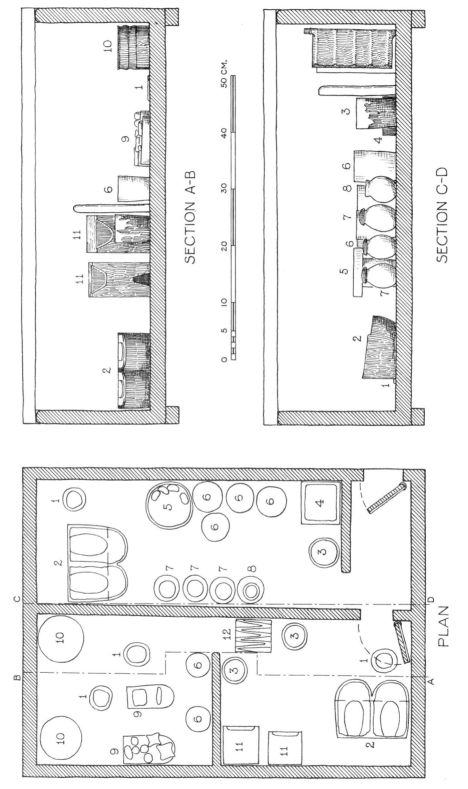

SECTION A-B

SECTION C-D

PLAN

64. The Brewery and Bakery (G)

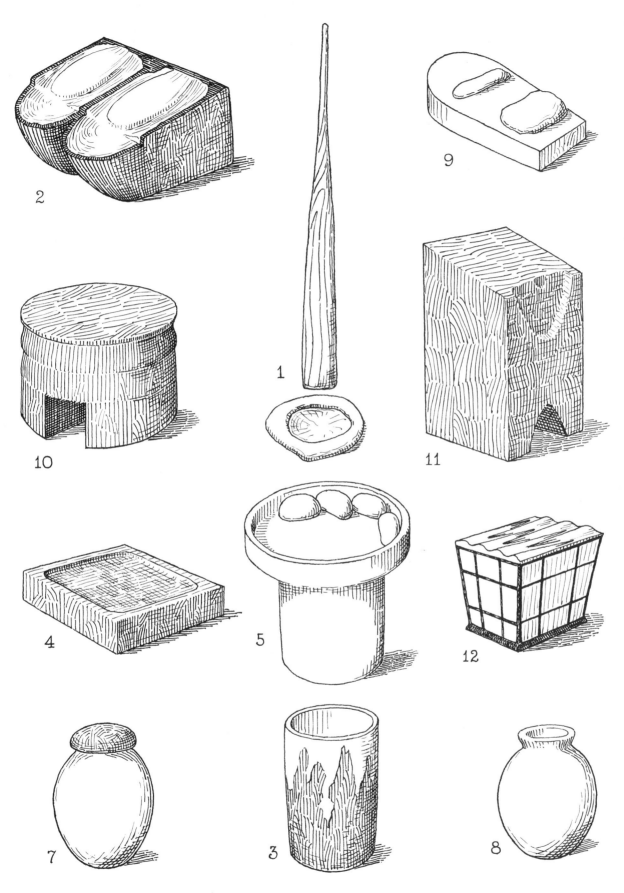

65. Equipment of the Brewery and Bakery (G)

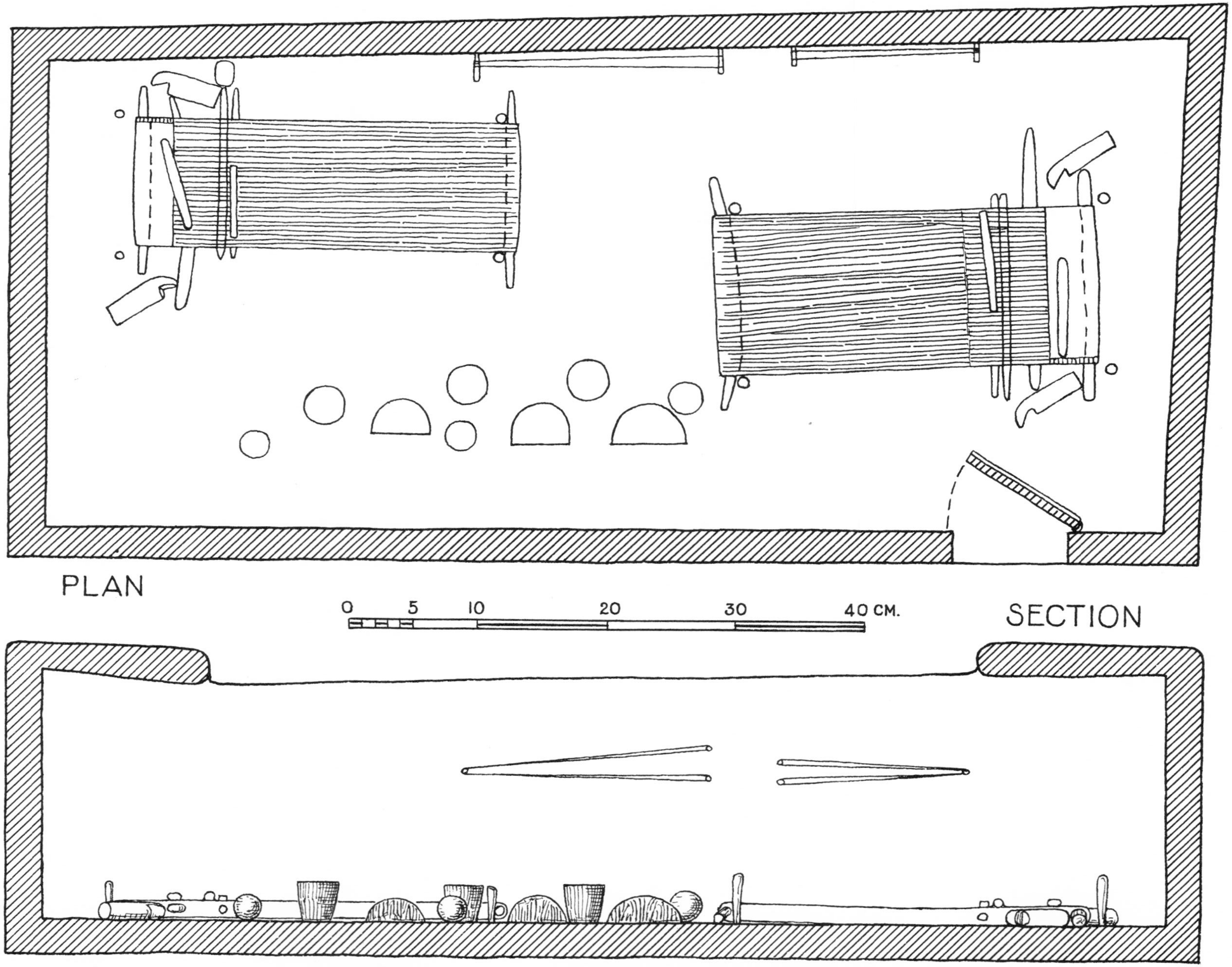

SECTION

PLAN

40 CM.

66. The Weaving Shop (H)

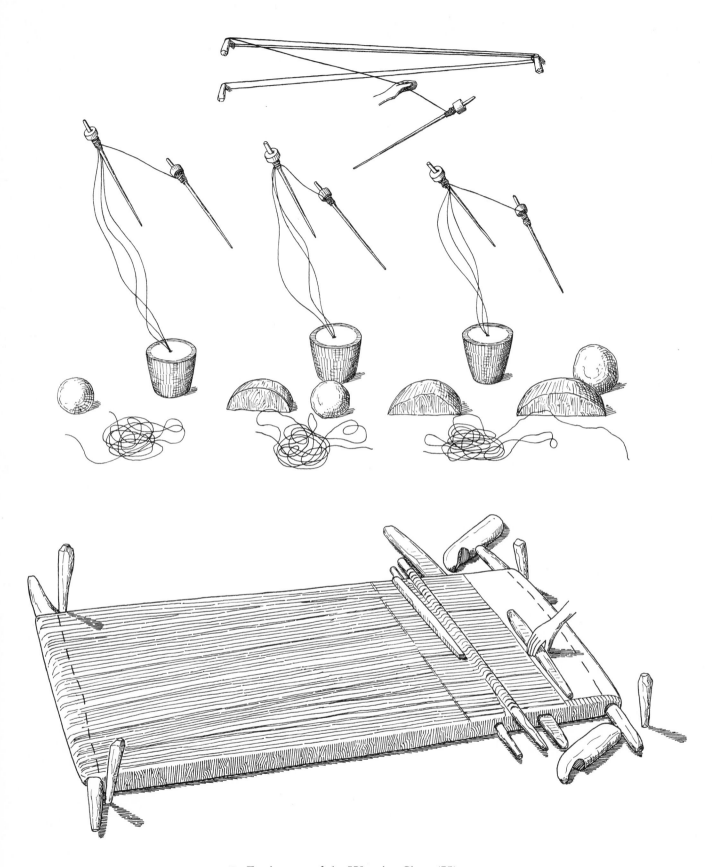

67. Equipment of the Weaving Shop (H)

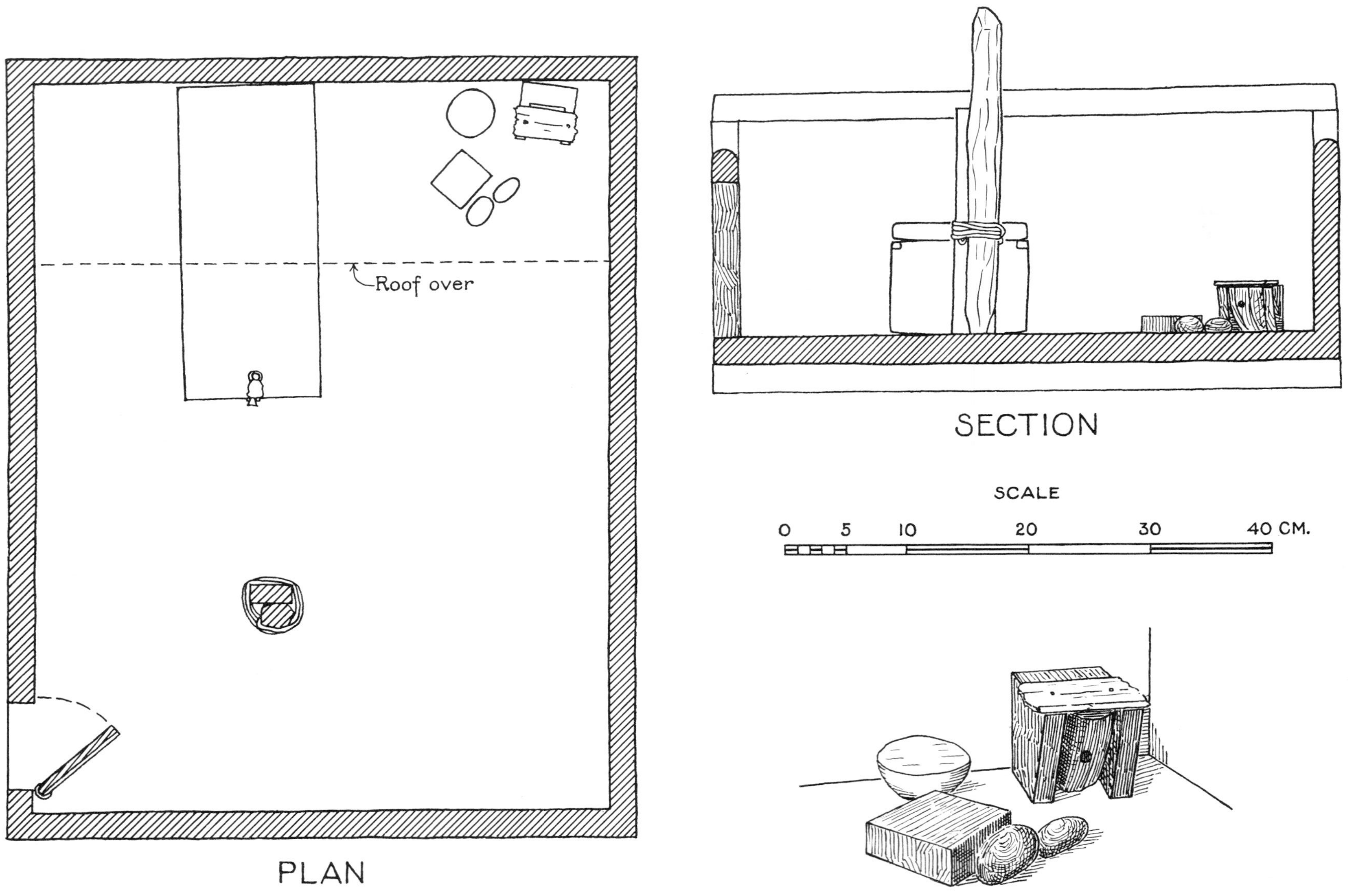

SECTION

SCALE

0 5 10 20 30 40 CM.

PLAN

Roof over

68. The Carpenter Shop (J)

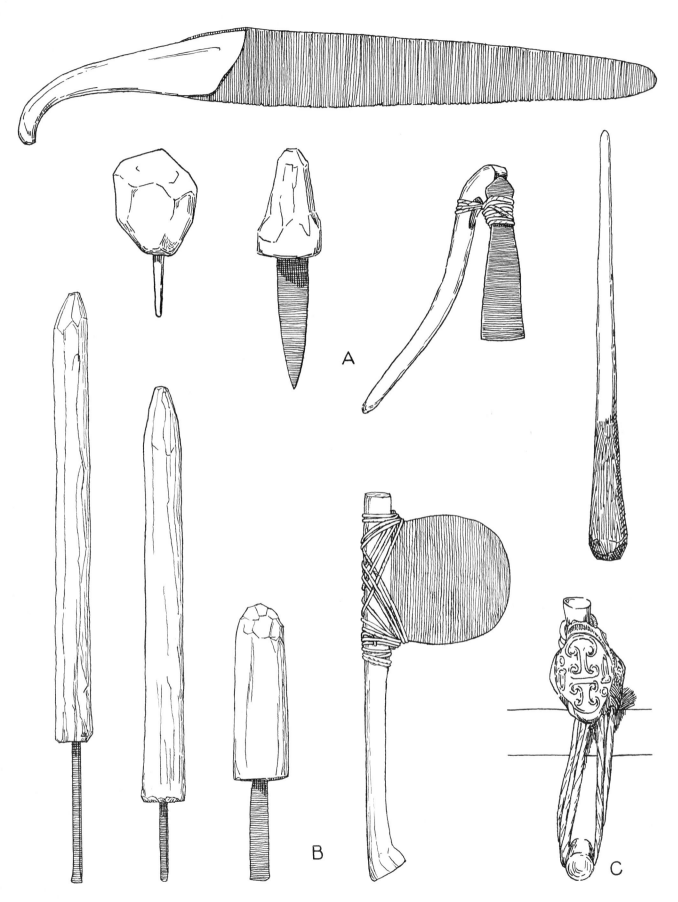

69. Equipment of the Carpenter Shop (J)

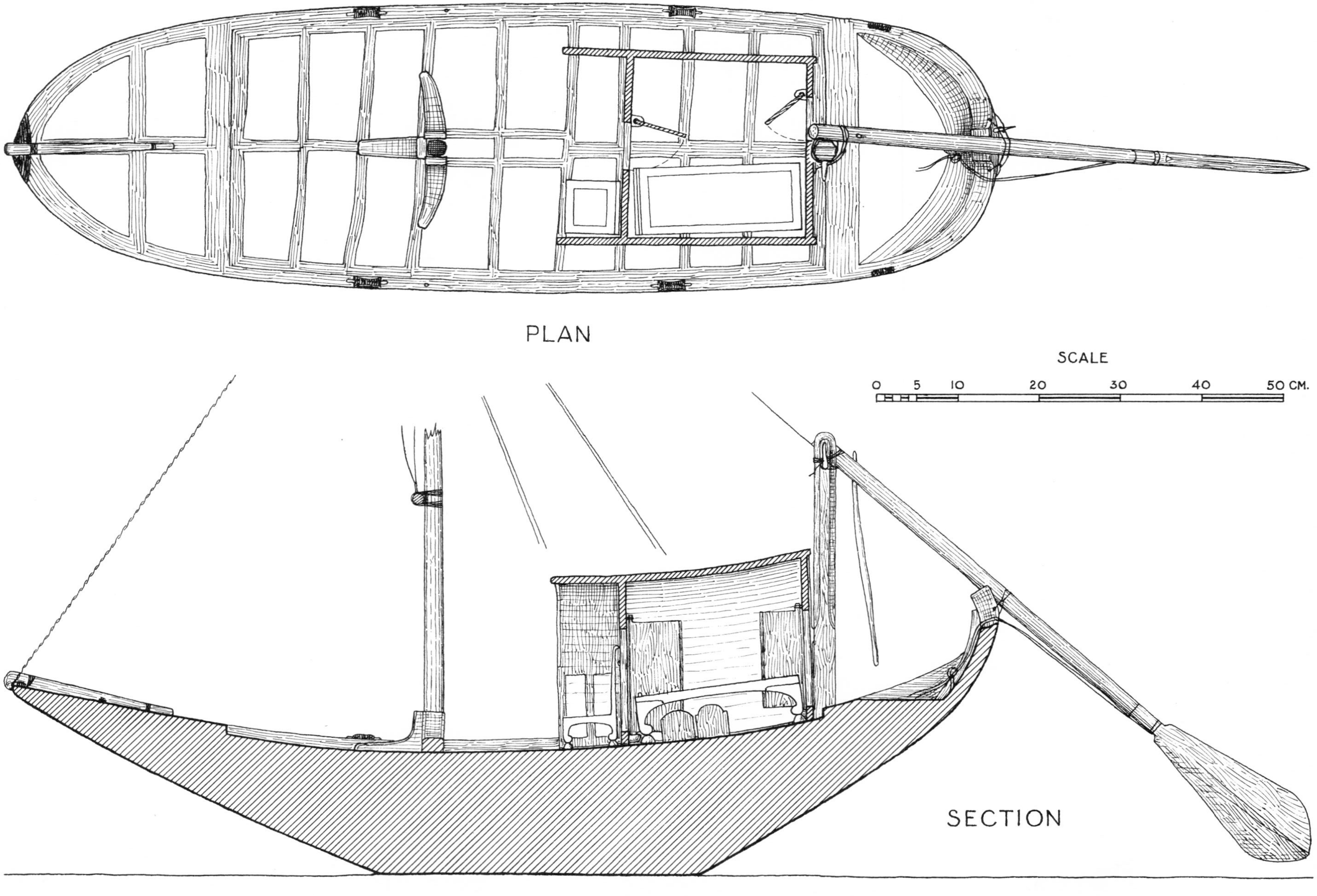

SCALE

CM. 0 5 10 20 30 40 50 CM.

PLAN

SECTION

70. Traveling Boat N

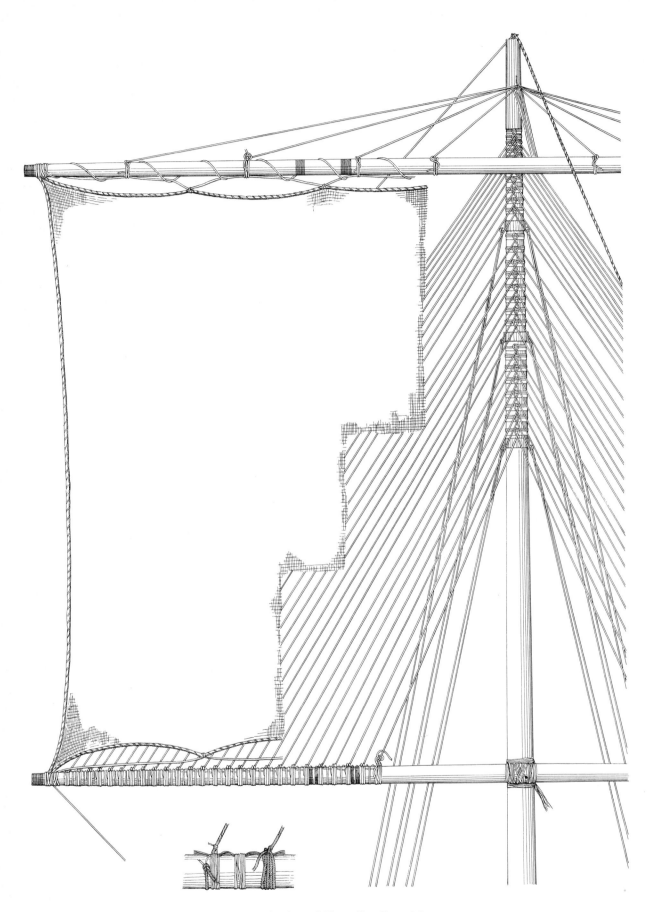

71. Rigging of Traveling Boat N

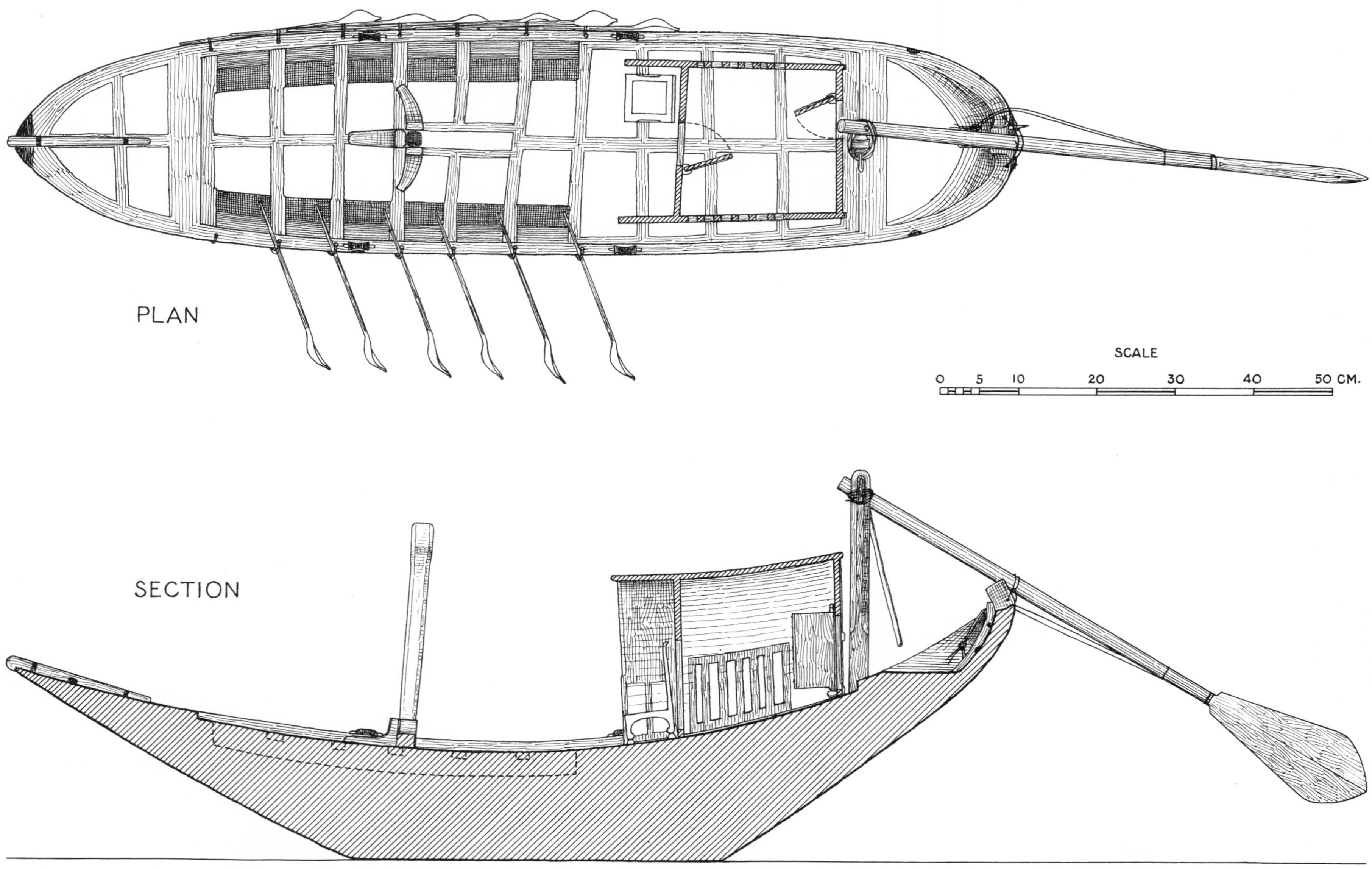

SCALE

0 5 10   20   30   40   50 CM.

PLAN

SECTION

72. Traveling Boat O

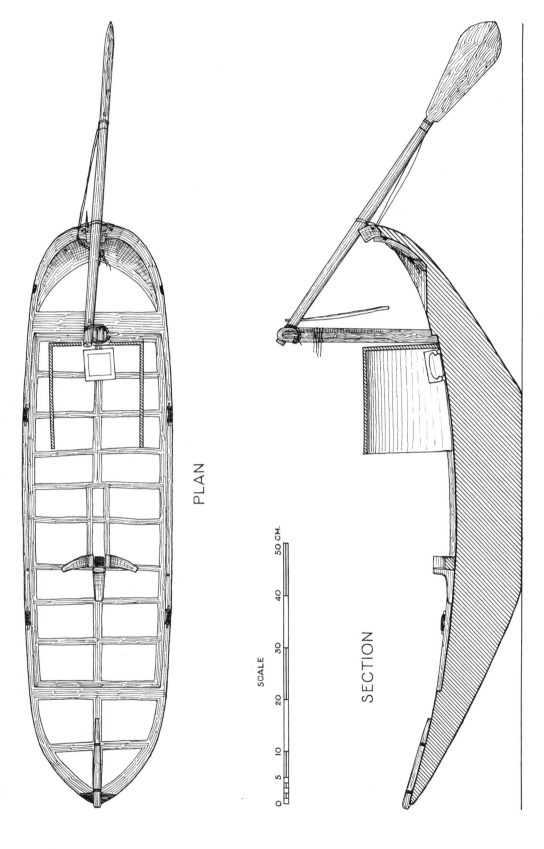

PLAN

SECTION

SCALE

0 5 10 20 30 40 50 CM.

73. Traveling Boat P

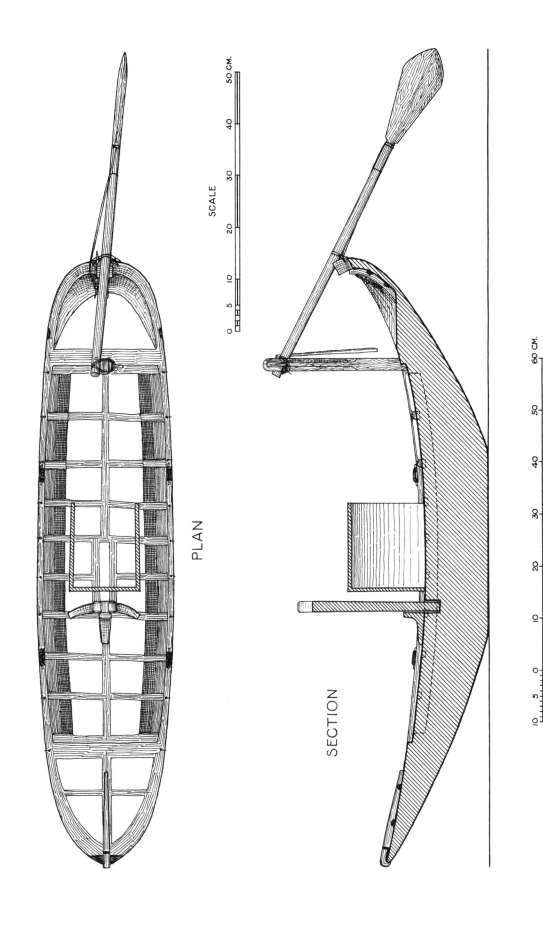

PLAN

SCALE

50 CM.

40

30

SCALE

20

10

5

0

SECTION

60 CM.

50

40

30

20

10

0

5

10

74. Traveling Boat Q

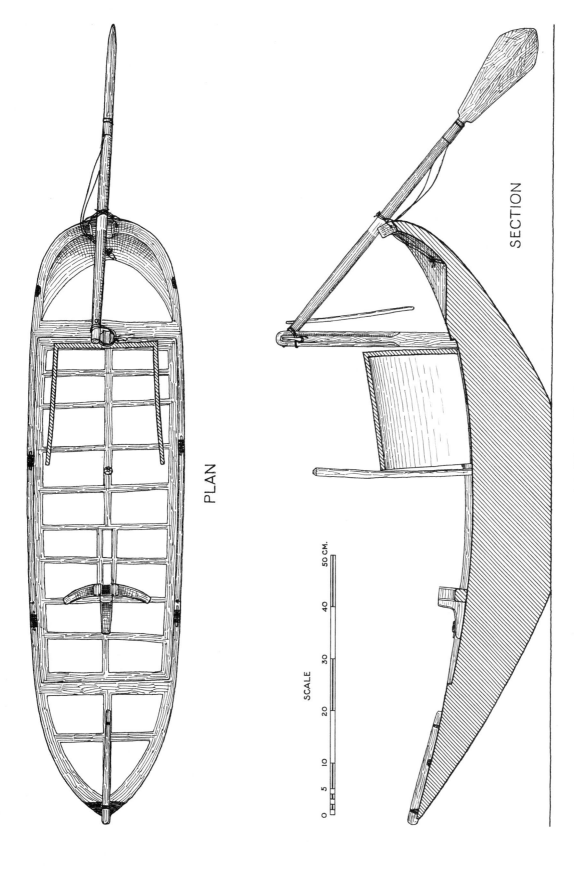

PLAN

SECTION

SCALE

0 5 10   20   30   40   50 CM.

75. Kitchen Tender R

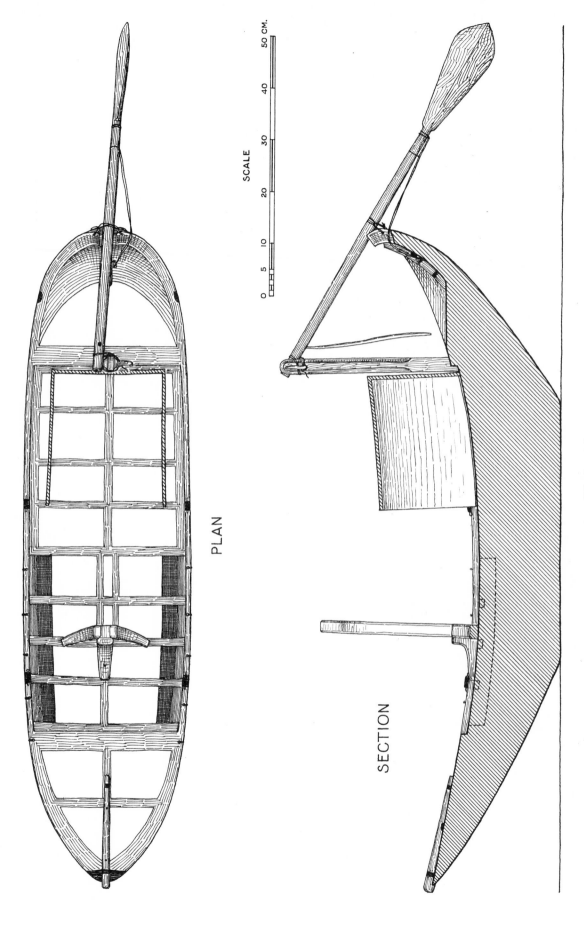

PLAN

SECTION

SCALE

O 5 10   20   30   40   50 CM.

76. Kitchen Tender S

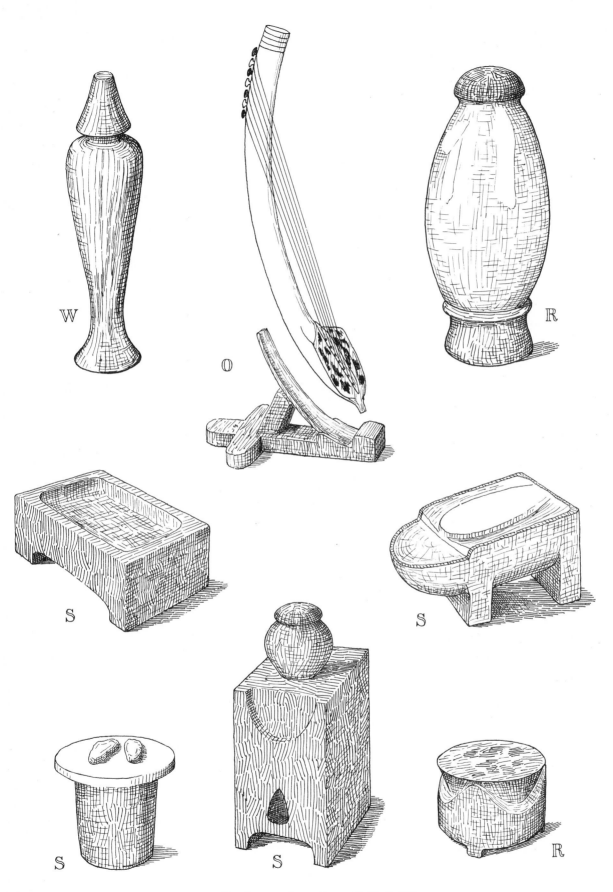

77. Equipment from Boats O, R, S, W

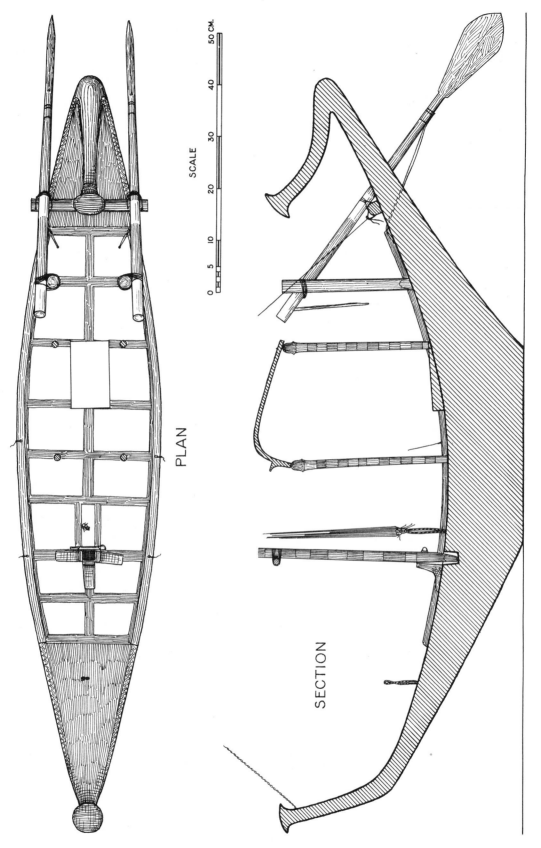

SCALE

50 CM.   40   30   20   10   5   0

PLAN

SECTION

78. Yacht T

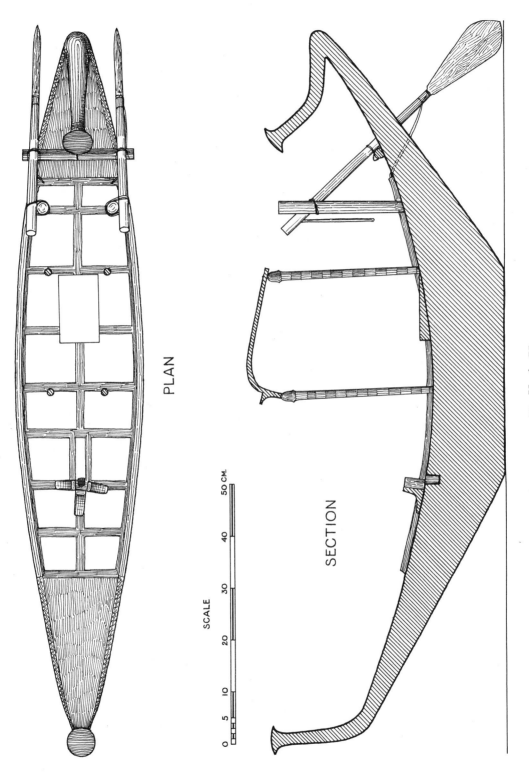

PLAN

SECTION

SCALE

0 5 10 20 30 40 50 CM.

79. Yacht U

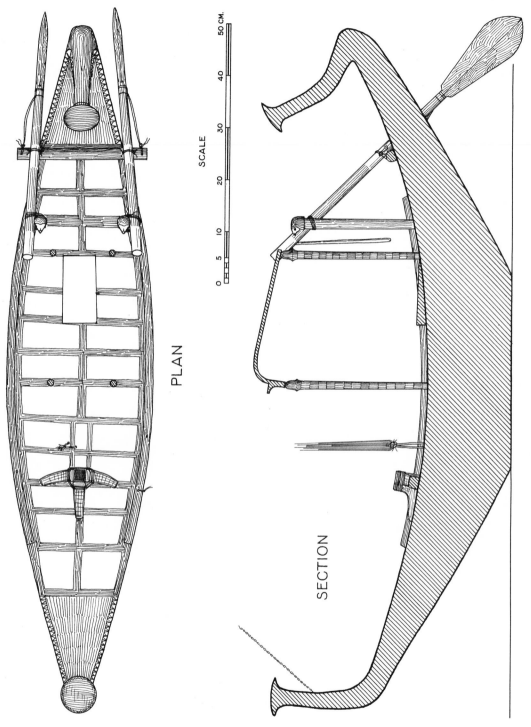

PLAN

SCALE

50 CM.

40

30

20

10

5

0

SECTION

80. Yacht V

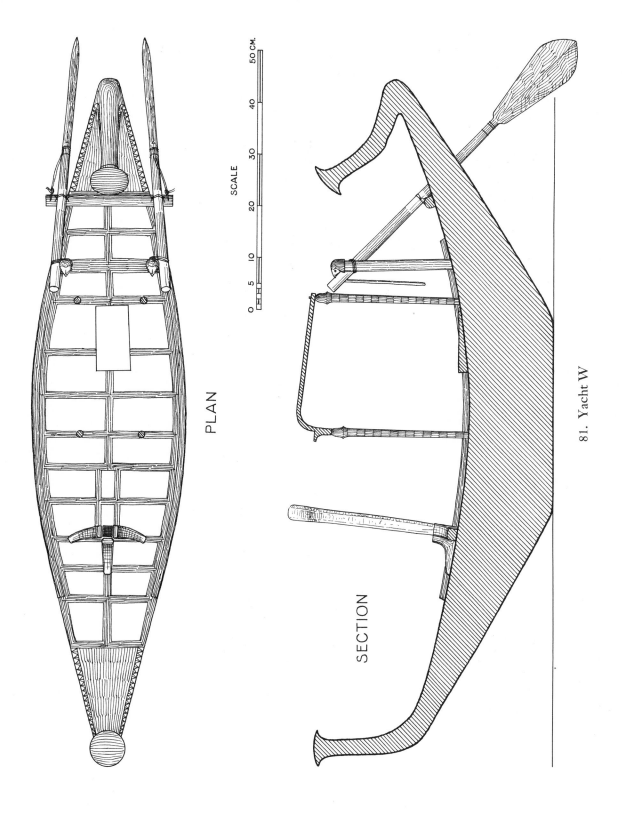

PLAN

SCALE

0   5   10   20   30   40   50 CM.

SECTION

81. Yacht W

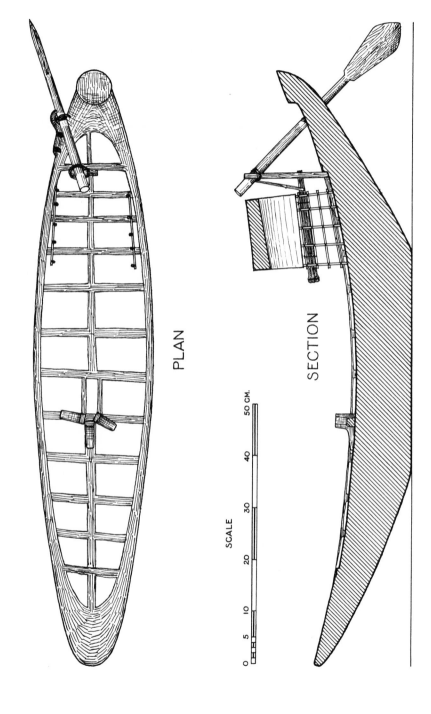

PLAN

SECTION

SCALE

0 5 10   20   30   40   50 CM.

82. The Sporting Boat (X)

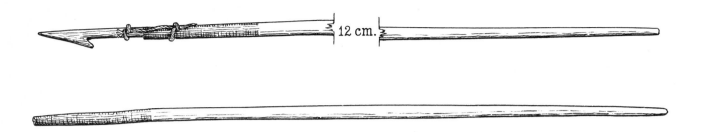

12 cm.

83. Equipment from the Sporting Boat (X)

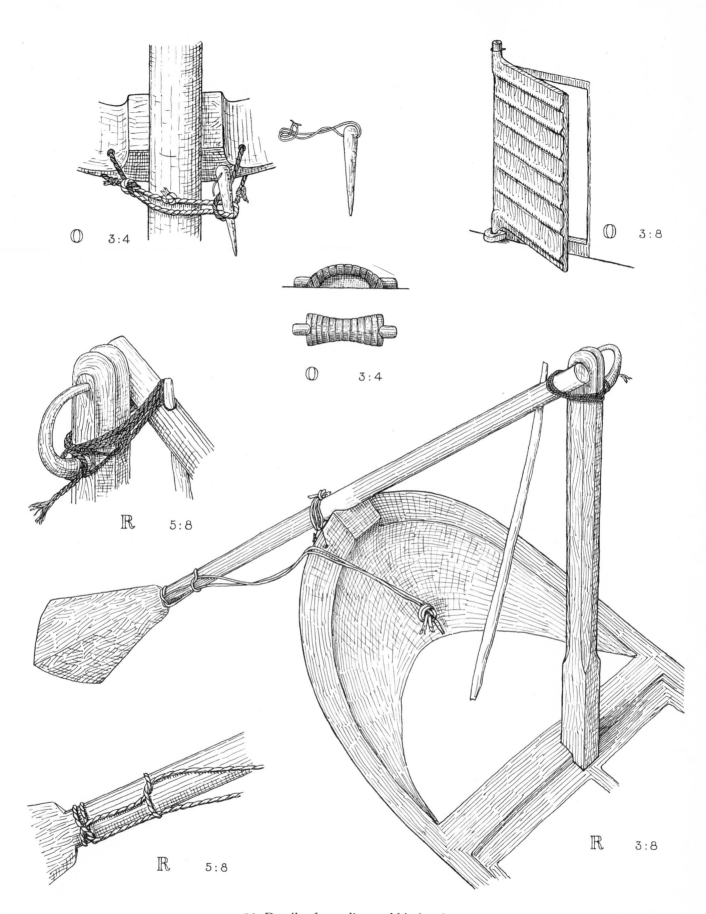

O   3:4

O   3:8

O   3:4

R   5:8

R   5:8

R   3:8

84. Details of traveling and kitchen boats

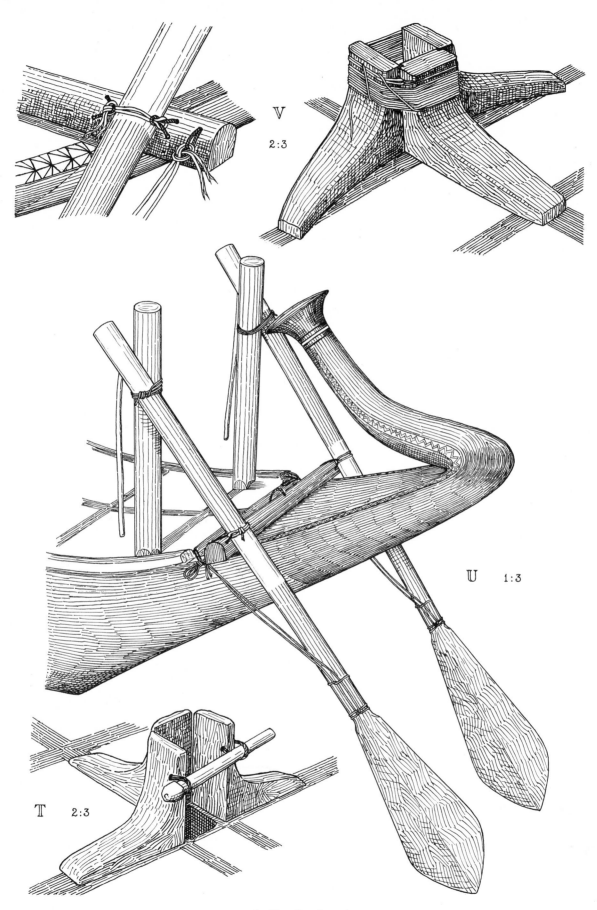

V 2:3

U 1:3

T 2:3

85. Details of yachts